MORE
RECIPES FROM
HOUR MAGAZINE

MORE
RECIPES FROM
HOUR MAGAZINE

Gary Collins

EDITOR: Catherine R. Pomponio
EXECUTIVE EDITOR: Martin M. Berman

G. P. PUTNAM'S SONS
NEW YORK

G. P. Putnam's Sons
Publishers Since 1838
200 Madison Avenue
New York, NY 10016

Permissions for recipes granted by presenter unless otherwise indicated

Photographs by Michael Leshnov, Paul Nichols

Library of Congress Cataloging-in-Publication Data

More recipes from Hour magazine/[selected by] Gary Collins; editor,
    Catherine R. Pomponio, executive editor, Martin M. Berman.—1st
    American ed.

    p. cm.
    Includes index.
    ISBN 0-399-13391-7
    1. Cookery. I. Collins, Gary, date. II. Pomponio, Catherine R.
    III. Hour magazine.
    TX714.M67   1988   88-23983 CIP
    641.5—dc19

Printed in the United States of America
1 2 3 4 5 6 7 8 9 10

To the memory of Bert Greene,
chef, author, and friend.
He will be deeply missed.

Special Thanks to . . .

First and foremost to Chris Circosta, chief propmaster, to whom we dedicated the first book and who continues to be the "master chef" and "most valuable player" in the *Hour* kitchen.

To Yvonne Collier Alvarez for organizing, researching, and putting this book together so efficiently and so cheerfully.

To Chris DeMore, whose conscientiousness had her laboring over the computer for days to be sure that everything was accurate.

To Jennifer Kemp, whose efficiency and sense of humor helped get us all through.

To Randy Jones, for his great investigating.

To Dan Sterchele, in audience relations, who keeps track of all the recipes we've done on the show and organizes them for our monthly volumes.

To Dr. David Sobel, director of patient education and health promotion for Kaiser Permanente in northern California, Myrna DeMartino, manager of the Regional Nutritional Services, and the registered dieticians who reviewed each of the recipes that follow.

And with thanks to Gene Brissie, our editor, who may not believe that we do deliver a daily television show on *time* day after day.

And of course, to the millions of viewers who continue to request recipes over the years.

And finally to the entire crew and staff for their contributions. Here's a list of a staff that truly deserves my thanks and your recognition—credits pass by each week all too quickly:

EXECUTIVE PRODUCER	DIRECTOR	SENIOR PRODUCER
Martin M. Berman	Morris Abraham	Laurence R. Ferber

PRODUCERS
Linda Bell
Karen Grace Cadle
Catherine R. Pomponio
Dan Weaver

COORDINATING PRODUCER
Carole Chouinard

TALENT COORDINATORS
Claudia Cagan
Carol Uchita

ASSOCIATE DIRECTOR
Barry Stoddard

ASSISTANT TO THE PRODUCERS
Allison L. Birnie

ASSOCIATE PRODUCERS
Jan Bisgaard
Linda Callahan
Carolyn DeRiggi
Kathy O'Reilly

PRODUCTION STAFF
Yvonne Alvarez
Michele Burns
Chris DeMore
Randy Jones
Jennifer Kemp
Dan Sterchele

UNIT PUBLICIST
Maureen Poon-Fear

ON-AIR PROMOTIONS
David G. Avalos

CONTRACT COORDINATOR
Stephanie Modory

DIRECTOR OF CREATIVE SERVICES
Paul Nichols

PRODUCTION MANAGER
Kevin E. Fortson

Table of Contents

3. RECIPE CONTEST WINNERS 167

4. YOUNG GOURMETS 175

5. *HOUR* FAMILY IN THE KITCHEN 185

6. SOUND NUTRITION 211

Introduction

When we put together the first *Hour Magazine* cookbook we were responding to the audience's encouragement to put all of the recipes made on the show into one volume. I'm so happy, three years later, to be able to sit down again and think back about the fun we've had and the recipes we've presented. I still seem to be answering questions about my positive response to so many meals. But I can honestly say, they're usually great!

What really made me excited about putting this volume together was the changes I've noticed in all the recipes we've been presenting on the show. They seemed to be healthier and more nutritious and so we went to Kaiser Permanente's* registered dieticians in the Northern California region and asked them to rate and review *every* recipe in the book. We were delighted that so many of them were highly rated by the experts.

So beside the recipes that received the highest ratings for what they consider "heart healthy," there'll be a symbol identifying them like this ♥ ♥. And beside those that were considered moderately healthy there'll be a symbol like this ♥.

What follows are some comments from the dieticians at Kaiser Permanente.

"Heart healthy" is defined as food items which are low in dairy fat, prepared with mono/unsaturated fat or oil, and with a minimum or void of egg yolk.

All meats are lean, with no restriction to the type of meat other than duck, goose, or other extremely high-fat meats such as sausage or bacon.

All foods are generally lower in sodium.

General Guidelines for Following a "Heart Healthy" Diet

- Select a margarine made from corn or safflower oil. Use these same oils when cooking.
- Select dairy products made from nonfat milk.
- Trim all fat from meat and poultry before cooking.
- Choose commercial salad dressings which are lower in fat and made from corn, soy, safflower, and olive oil.
- Eat fresh fruits or desserts made with appropriate oils and dairy products in place of creamy pastries and pies.

*Kaiser Permanente is the largest and one of the best HMOs (health maintanence organizations) in the country.

- Limit egg yolks to two per week.
- Limit foods high in salt.

By following these guidelines, you may be able to alter your family's meals and create a healthier diet.

Because we noticed that so many of the recipes were concerned with good nutrition, we've included a whole chapter with information from Dr. Rosenfeld, Dr. Sobel, and many of the nutritionists we continue to invite back to *Hour Magazine*.

We're in the middle of our ninth year of programming and we're so glad to still be a part of your lives. We're pleased you enjoy the cooking segments as much as we do—because there's still some truth in the words of the Earl of Lytton, Edward Robert Bulwer-Lytton, who said way back in 1860:

> We may live without poetry, music, and art;
> We may live without conscience, and live without heart;
> We may live without friends; we may live without books;
> But civilized man cannot live without cooks.

And so to the cooks—enjoy!

Gary Collins

1

CHEFS, GASTRONOMES, AND RESTAURATEURS

Over the years, the cooking spots that are the most well received are those of bona fide chefs who have restaurants and cookbooks themselves. I always enjoy working with them because they are such professionals, and I usually learn a practical cooking tip during the demonstration. Here are some of our favorite chefs and their recipes over the past few years.

BARBARA Albright is the editor-in-chief of *Chocolatier* magazine, and she says she was allowed to mess up the kitchen and experiment at a very early age. As editor-in-chief, her goal is to delight her readers with one of life's greatest indulgences—chocolate and desserts. Her Low-Calorie Chocolate Sauce and Chocolate Banana Shake recipes are simple-to-follow desserts.

♥ ♥ Low-Calorie Chocolate Sauce

⅓ cup nonalkalized cocoa powder
⅓ cup dark brown sugar, packed
2 teaspoons cornstarch
1 cup water
1½ teaspoons vanilla extract

In a medium saucepan, stir together the cocoa powder, brown sugar, and cornstarch until combined. Stir in the water and heat over medium-high heat, stirring constantly until the mixture comes to a boil. Continue to boil and stir for 1 minute, until the sauce thickens. Stir in the vanilla.

Variations:

· Flavored liqueurs can also be used in place of the vanilla for extra pizzazz.
· For a calorie-controlled chocolaty treat, serve the sauce over fresh fruit, angel food cake, ice milk, or sorbet. It can also be used in the recipe for Chocolate Banana Shake.

Makes 1½ cups of sauce
20 calories per tablespoon of sauce

BARBARA ALBRIGHT

Chocolate Banana Shake

1 small banana
1 cup skim milk
1½ tablespoons Low-Calorie Chocolate Sauce

¼ teaspoon vanilla extract
3 ice cubes

In the container of a blender, process all of the ingredients until combined. Serve immediately.

Makes 1 shake
227 calories per serving

Reprinted by permission of Barbara Albright, editor-in-chief of *Chocolatier* Magazine and co-author with Leslie Weiner of *Mostly Muffins, Simply Scones* and *Wild About Brownies.* Copyright © 1986.

ANNETTE Annechild is a food and fitness writer living in California. Her latest book, *Steam Cuisine,* has made cooking for busy health-conscious cooks easier than ever. Steamed foods are high in nutritive value and low in fat and calories. And all you need for these recipes is a large covered pot and a rack or steamer!

Garden Parmesan Omelet

8 eggs
½ onion, chopped
¼ teaspoon dried oregano
Pepper to taste
½ cup grated Parmesan cheese
½ cup bean sprouts
1 tomato, sliced
¼ cucumber, sliced
Parmesan cheese to sprinkle on top

Lightly beat the eggs in a mixing bowl.
Add onion, oregano, pepper, Parmesan cheese, and bean sprouts. Stir to blend.
Pour egg mixture into a buttered 1½-quart casserole dish.
Top with tomato and cucumber slices. Sprinkle with extra Parmesan cheese.

20 MORE RECIPES FROM HOUR MAGAZINE

Place casserole dish on a steaming rack over boiling water in a pot or wok; cover tightly. Steam for 25 to 30 minutes, or until a knife comes out clean when inserted. Check water level during cooking time, adding more if needed. Serve immediately.

Serves 6

ANNETTE ANNECHILD

♥ ## Raspberry Steamer Cakes

      2 cups fresh raspberries
      2 cups unbleached white flour
      4 teaspoons baking powder
    ½ teaspoon salt
      1 cup sugar
      4 tablespoons soybean margarine, butter, or margarine
      2 eggs, well beaten
      1 cup milk

Clean raspberries; set aside.
Mix flour, baking powder, salt, and sugar.
Cut in margarine or butter with a knife or pastry blender.
Add the eggs, raspberries, and milk.
Pour into 6 well-greased custard cups.
Place cups on a steaming rack over boiling water in a wok or pot. Cover and steam for 90 minutes. Check water level occasionally, adding more as needed.
Unmold and enjoy!

Makes 6 cakes

ANNETTE ANNECHILD

Reprinted by permission of Macmillan Publishing Company from *Steam Cuisine* by Annette Annechild. Copyright © 1987 by Annette Annechild.

PERINO'S is one of the legendary restaurants in Los Angeles. And even though many Italian restaurants are cropping up all over the city, there is only one PERINO'S. We invited owner Carlo Bondanelli to spend some time in *Hour* kitchen. Naturally he brought a man he cannot do without, pasta chef **Marcello Apollonio**. And here are two "authentic" PERINO'S' recipes that are bound to become a part of your permanent collection!

Manicotti Four Cheeses

Filling

4 ounces Swiss cheese
4 ounces fontina or similar cheese
4 ounces Edam
3 ounces sweet butter
3 ounces flour
2 cups milk
1 egg yolk
Salt
2 ounces fresh grated Parmesan

Crêpe

4 ounces flour
3 whole eggs
1 cup milk
Béchamel for Manicotti (recipe follows)

Prepare the filling: Dice the Swiss, fontina, and Edam cheeses.

In a frying pan melt the butter and gradually add the flour. Mix well and add the diced cheese; keep stirring on medium heat, pouring in the milk slowly and gradually. Keep stirring until the cheese has melted.

Add the yolk, salt to taste, and 1 ounce grated Parmesan cheese. Stir until you get a perfectly blended paste.

Prepare the crêpe: Put the crêpe ingredients in a bowl and stir until you get a uniform liquid blend.

Prepare a shallow crêpe pan: Grease with butter and warm it well.

Pour the crêpe mix to form a thin layer to cover the pan. Let fry for 20 to 25 seconds; turn the crêpe and let fry for 15 to 20 seconds. Remove the crêpe from the pan and open it on the table.

Form the cheese stuffing into a loaf and roll up once in crêpe. Cut the roll into desired-size slices, and put in a skillet on a bed of béchamel. Cover at random with more béchamel and sprinkle with the remaining ounce of grated Parmesan. Bake in 350° oven for 15 minutes.

Serves 6

PERINO'S

Béchamel for Manicotti

2 ounces sweet butter
1 ounce flour
10 ounces milk
Salt
Nutmeg

Put butter and flour in a pan and mix well on medium heat. When all is blended, increase heat.

In a separate pan, boil the milk. When milk is boiling pour on the mixture, stir and bring to a boil. Turn heat to low and stir occasionally for 10 minutes. Add salt and a shade of nutmeg.

PERINO'S

♥ ♥ ## Spaghetti Lido

2 tablespoons rock salt
12 ounces eggplant, peeled
Cooking oil
10 ounces swordfish
2 pounds ripe fresh tomatoes
5–6 leaves fresh basil
4–5 leaves fresh mint
3 cloves garlic
1 glass dry white wine (approximately 5 ounces)
Salt and pepper
1 pound spaghetti (preferably De Cecco)
Virgin olive oil

Start boiling 1½ gallons water (add approximately 2 tablespoons rock salt), ready for spaghetti.

Dice the eggplant and fry lightly, using 2 to 3 tablespoons cooking oil.

Dice the swordfish, peel and dice the tomatoes, and chop the basil and mint leaves.

In a large shallow pan approximately 15 inches in diameter, fry the cloves of garlic in 2 to 3 tablespoons cooking oil, until they reach a light brown color, then add the diced swordfish and the white wine. Let cook on moderate heat for 2 to 3 minutes, stirring occasionally.

Add the fried eggplant, the diced tomatoes, and the chopped basil and mint leaves. Add salt and/or pepper to taste.

Let cook for approximately 3 minutes, stirring occasionally.

During the sauce preparation start cooking the spaghetti, making sure that the water is fully boiling. Keep the sauce warm; if it seems too thick, add ½ glass of the boiling water.

Cook spaghetti at a full boil for 5 minutes, strain, and pour in the large pan, stirring to make sure that the spaghetti is mixed well with the sauce.

Turn off the burner, add 2 to 3 tablespoons virgin olive oil, and serve.

Serves 6

PERINO'S

MARY Anne Bauer, chef from Seattle and author of *Simply Entertaining*, gives us a basic recipe for waffles that are crisp on the outside, soft on the inside, and light as air, with suggestions for variations and simple butters.

Waffles

2 cups sifted flour
3 teaspoons baking powder
2 tablespoons sugar
1 teaspoon salt
3 egg yolks, beaten
1¼ cups milk
4 tablespoons melted shortening
3 egg whites, beaten until stiff

Sift flour, baking powder, sugar, and salt into medium bowl. Mix beaten egg yolks, milk, and shortening in separate bowl. Beat thoroughly.

Add to dry ingredients, stirring lightly until mixed. Fold in beaten egg whites gently. Bake 3 to 4 minutes in a hot waffle iron.

Variations

- Apple waffles. Add 1 teaspoon cinnamon with dry ingredients. Add 1 cup chopped raw apple to batter. Serve with cinnamon-and-sugar and butter. Serve with orange maple syrup.
- Blueberry waffles. Add 1 cup fresh or frozen blueberries to dry ingredients. A half teaspoon cinnamon is a nice flavor accent. Serve with blueberry syrup.
- Chocolate waffles. Add ½ cup cocoa and increase sugar to ¼ cup. Sift with dry ingredients. Serve with whipped cream.
- Nut waffles. Add 2 teaspoons chopped nuts to dry ingredients. Serve with orange maple syrup.
- Orange waffles. Add 1 teaspoon grated orange rind to batter and substitute ½ cup orange juice for ½ cup milk. Serve with orange maple syrup.

Makes 5 to 6 waffles

MARY ANNE BAUER

Strawberry Butter

¾ cup frozen strawberries, drained
1 cup soft butter
3 tablespoons powdered sugar

In a small bowl mix strawberries, butter, and sugar well. Serve with muffins, fruit bread, or rolls.

Makes 1½ cups

MARY ANNE BAUER

Honey Butter

½ cup (1 stick) butter
3 tablespoons honey

In a small bowl, mix butter and honey well.
Serve with biscuits.

Makes about ¾ cup

MARY ANNE BAUER

Reprinted by permission of Mary Anne Bauer from *Simply Entertaining.* Copyright ©
1984 Mary Anne Bauer Productions.

ALLEN Bernstein, who since 1982 has been chairman of the board
and chief executive officer of Le Peep Restaurants, Inc., located
in New York, came in to cook some extraordinary breakfasts. The two
recipes we've included are great for a weekend brunch.

Zapata Frittata

6 ounces whipped eggs (4 eggs)
2 ounces cooked chorizo sausage
2 tablespoons diced jalapeños
¼ cup diced green peppers
2 tablespoons diced onion
2 tablespoons warm salsa
2 ounces grated cheddar and Monterey Jack cheeses

Pour whipped eggs into a buttered 8-inch skillet over medium heat. Add
chorizo, jalapeños, green pepper, and onion. Cook until eggs set. Drain uncooked
egg underneath cooked egg by lifting the edges with a rubber spatula. Flip or turn
frittata over in skillet and cook briefly. Cover frittata with salsa and grated cheese.
Melt cheese under a heated broiler. Lift or slide onto a plate, and top with sour
cream and chives. Serve with breakfast potatoes and English muffin.

Serves 2

ALLEN BERNSTEIN

Bumper Crop

5 ounces whipped eggs (3–4 eggs)
Butter
½ cup chopped broccoli and water chestnuts
¼ cup sliced mushrooms
2 ounces cream cheese
Dillweed (to taste)
Broccoli sprig
Hollandaise

Pour 5 ounces whipped eggs into a buttered skillet over medium heat. Add chopped broccoli, water chestnuts, sliced mushrooms, cream cheese, and a pinch of dillweed. Stir while cooking to create a velvety appearance. Place in a rarebit dish; garnish with a sprig of broccoli and a side dish of hollandaise. Serve with breakfast potatoes and English muffin.

Serves 2

ALLEN BERNSTEIN

AMERICANS consume approximately 3 billion pounds of pasta a year. And some Italians believe that pasta is not only great for dinner but is wonderful to wake up to. **Elisa Celli,** whose latest book is *Italian Light Cooking,* is a food consultant, gourmet writer, and critic. She has also operated a chain of cooking schools. Here's one of her great breakfast pastas.

Breakfast Capellini

2 tablespoons sweet butter
½ pound capellini or angel hair pasta, cooked and tossed
    with olive oil
4 egg whites
¼ cup chopped pimento pepper
¼ cup chopped parsley

½ cup minced prosciutto or other ham
¼ cup grated Parmesan cheese

Heat butter in skillet. Add cooked pasta. Add egg whites; cook 2 minutes, stirring constantly. Add remaining ingredients. Toss thoroughly.

Serves 2

ELISA CELLI

WHO could forget a visit from **Myra Chanin,** also known as "Mother Wonderful." And though she has been recognized for her exquisite cheesecakes, she's been branching out and cooking great vegetable dishes as well. Here are two recipes that say it all.

Mother Wonderful's Vegetable Kugel

6 tablespoons margarine
1½ cups grated carrots
½ cup coarsely chopped red peppers
1 cup coarsely chopped scallions (white and about 3" of green)
½ cup coarsely chopped fennel (or celery)
One 10-ounce package frozen chopped spinach, defrosted
3 large eggs, lightly beaten
1 teaspoon salt (or more to taste)
½ teaspoon white pepper
¾ cup unsalted matzo meal (or breadcrumbs)

Preheat oven to 350°.
Melt margarine in a skillet. Sauté carrots, peppers, scallions, and fennel until soft. Remove from heat, then add chopped spinach. *Do not press the excess water out of the spinach. Include it in the kugel.* Let cool slightly, then add eggs, salt, and pepper. Mix in matzo meal well. Bake in a greased square baking pan for 40 to 45 minutes. This kugel can easily be doubled and quadrupled, and will cook in about the same time.

Variations

Instead of chopped spinach, you can use fresh watercress or fresh arugula chopped in comparable amounts.

Serves 6

MYRA CHANIN

Instant No-Bake Pumpkin Cheesecake

Crust

1 cup very finely ground crumbs from ginger snaps
2 tablespoons finely ground walnuts
2 tablespoons sugar
2 ounces lightly salted butter, melted over low heat

Combine all ingredients for crust until well blended. Press mixture up sides first, then on bottom of an ungreased pan—a 9-inch springform preferably, but almost anything will do. If you run short of crust, grind up a few more cookies and fill in the holes on the bottom. Place in refrigerator.

Batter

12 ounces cream cheese
½ teaspoon rum or rum extract
½ teaspoon brandy or brandy extract
¾ teaspoon ground cinnamon
    Pinch ground nutmeg
⅓ cup frozen undiluted orange juice
1 tablespoon fresh lemon juice
1 can sweetened condensed milk
1 cup canned pumpkin
⅛ teaspoon ground mace
2 tablespoons maple syrup

Blend batter ingredients in food processor.
When all blended, add ¼ cup chopped walnuts, English or black and 2 tablespoons thinly sliced crystallized ginger and mix in.
Pour into crust or bowl, put in the refrigerator, and let set.

Topping

½ cup whipping cream
1 tablespoon confectioners' sugar
1 teaspoon brandy

Whip topping ingredients together.
Fill pastry bag fitted with star tube. Cover with rosettes.
Put topping on about 2 hours before cake is to be served.
Sprinkle with finely chopped crystallized ginger.

Serves 6 to 8

MYRA CHANIN

ANN Clark, who runs LA BONNE CUISINE, a successful cooking school in Austin, Texas, has also been a consultant to restaurants across the country. When she came to *Hour Magazine,* she told me that she's discovered many people have a fear of fish. Her cookbook, *Fabulous Fish,* helps to overcome that fear. She made a great "whole fish" on our show.

♥ ♥ Baked Whole Fish à la Provençale

One 3 to 3½-pound whole sea bass, cleaned and scaled,
with head and tail left on

Marinade

1 tablespoon fennel seeds
1 teaspoon each thyme, rosemary, and summer savory
½ teaspoon each dried basil, dried oregano, and freshly ground black pepper
Pinch of dried sage
2 tablespoons salt
⅓ to ½ cup fresh lemon juice
½ cup extra-virgin olive oil
Sprigs of fresh thyme, rosemary, oregano, sage, or parsley for garnish

Rinse fish in cold water and wipe with a damp cloth. With a sharp knife, score the fish on both sides, cutting two or three large overlapping X's about ½ inch deep. Place fish in a glass or metal oval baking dish.

Crush the fennel, herbs, spices, and salt together in a mortar. Add lemon juice and stir to dissolve salt. Mix in olive oil. Pour this marinade over the scored fish and turn to coat well. Refrigerate, turning once, for 1 to 2 hours.

Bake the fish, uncovered, at 425°, allowing 10 minutes per inch of thickness (measure at thickest part), about 30 to 40 minutes. Baste fish several times with marinade. Test for doneness by inserting a small knife under the flesh at the backbone; if the fish is done, the flesh flakes easily and looks milky white, not gray and translucent.

To serve, place on a heated oval platter and, with a sharp knife and a serving spatula, make two or three vertical cuts across the fish. Slip the knife in at the backbone horizontally and slide the knife across the top of the bones from gills to tail to detach the flesh from the bones. Remove two or three neatly cut portions with spatula. Detach the spine at the base of the head with one sharp cut and remove to another plate. Make two or three more vertical cuts through the flesh and skin and serve, garnished with sprigs of fresh herbs.

Variation

- You can also use whole redfish, red snapper, pompano, porgy, drum, rockfish, or sheepshead. This dish is also good made with a large fillet of bluefish or a thick tuna or swordfish steak.

Serves 4 to 6

ANN CLARK

Reprinted by permission of Ann Clark from *Fabulous Fish*. Copyright © 1987 by Ann Clark, New American Library.

♥ ♥
Lamb Moghul

One 7- to 8-pound leg of spring lamb, butterflied

Marinade

   3 cups plain yogurt
     Juice of 6 limes
   2 teaspoons minced fresh ginger
4½ teaspoons coarse salt
1½ teaspoons cayenne pepper
   3 tablespoons coriander seeds
1½ teaspoons ground cinnamon
1½ teaspoons ground cloves
1½ teaspoons ground cardamom
   1 teaspoon freshly ground black pepper

Carefully cut away all the fat and tissue from the meat, and make several slits on both sides with a sharp knife. Put the lamb in a noncorrodible roasting pan.

Combine the marinade ingredients in a bowl and pour over the lamb. Cover and refrigerate for at least 2 days, turning the meat at least 3 or 4 times during this period.

Remove the lamb from the refrigerator and bring to room temperature. Prepare a large charcoal fire and, when the coals are medium-hot, remove the lamb from the marinade and grill it about 4 inches above the coals for 5 to 8 minutes on each side to sear and seal; then raise the grill several inches and grill for about 10 to 15 minutes.

Serves 6

SUSAN COSTNER

Spring Tonic

        2 cucumbers, peeled
        1 small carrot, peeled and finely grated
        2 scallions, white part only, finely chopped
        ¼ cup chopped fresh mint
        1 garlic clove, peeled
        1 quart plain yogurt or buttermilk
        1 pint sour cream
        1 teaspoon salt
        2 tablespoon freshly squeezed lemon juice
        ¾ cup club soda

Garnish

        Freshly ground black pepper
        Chopped fresh parsley

Cut 6 paper-thin slices from 1 cucumber and set them aside. Cut the cucumbers in half lengthwise; scoop out the seeds and discard them. Cut the cucumbers into small pieces.

In a blender or food processor, place half the chopped cucumber, half the grated carrot, half the scallions, half the mint, and all the garlic. Moisten with 2 cups yogurt and blend until smooth. Pour the pureed mixture into a large serving pitcher or bowl, and whisk in the remaining yogurt, sour cream, salt, and lemon juice. Fold in the remaining vegetables and mint. Cover and chill thoroughly.

Just before serving, stir in the club soda. Garnish each bowl or mug with a reserved cucumber slice, a grinding of pepper, and some chopped parsley.

Serves 6

SUSAN COSTNER

Reprinted by permission of Susan Costner from *Good Friends, Great Dinners* by Susan Costner. Copyright © 1987 by Crown Publishers, Inc.

Fig Pound Cake

2 cups all-purpose flour
½ cup yellow cornmeal
½ teaspoon salt
2 sticks butter, softened
1⅔ cups sugar
5 eggs
2 teaspoons vanilla extract
½ cup milk
1 cup dried calimyrna figs, chopped
½ cup pine nuts

Sauce

½ cup sugar
1 tablespoon cornstarch
3 tablespoons fresh lemon juice
2 tablespoons butter
Grated lemon rind
Salt

Make sauce: Combine sugar, cornstarch, and lemon juice in a small pan. Cook, stirring constantly, until thick and clear.

Remove from heat. Stir in butter, rind, and salt to taste. Set aside. Preheat oven to 350°.

Butter and flour an 8 × 4 × 2-inch loaf pan. Combine flour, cornmeal, and salt in a bowl; stir with fork to mix well.

Put butter in bowl, beat, and slowly add the sugar; blend well.

Add eggs to butter mixture, two at a time, and beat until light. Add flour mixture alternately with vanilla and milk; beat until smooth.

Stir in figs and nuts. Spoon into greased loaf pan; bake about 45 minutes, or until a straw comes out clean when inserted in center. Cool on rack. Slice thin to serve.

Variation

Omit figs and pine nuts; substitute ½ cup chopped citron and 1 tablespoon caraway seeds.

Serves 8 to 10

MARION CUNNINGHAM

Reprinted by permission of Marion Cunningham from The Breakfast Book by Marion Cunningham. Copyright © 1987 by Alfred A. Knopf, Inc.

MARY Emmerling was a food and decorating editor of *Mademoiselle, Self,* and *House Beautiful* and the author of *Mary Emmerling's American Country Cookbook.*

She came to *Hour*'s kitchen with some uniquely American recipes— and of course, indicated that serving them in the right bowls and dinnerware can enhance their taste!

Cream of Wild Mushroom Soup

    6 tablespoons (¾ stick) unsalted butter
 1½ pounds wild mushrooms, such as King Boletus, Meadow,
       or chanterelles
    1 medium onion, thinly sliced
  ½ cup all-purpose flour
       Three 14-ounce cans undiluted chicken broth, or 5¼
       cups homemade chicken stock
    1 tablespoon fresh lemon juice
  ¼ cup minced fresh parsley
    3 cups half-and-half
       Salt and freshly ground black pepper
  ½ cup dry vermouth

In a large heavy saucepan, melt the butter over moderate heat. Add the mushrooms and onion, and sauté until the vegetables are limp but not browned and all of the moisture has evaporated. Set aside to cool for a few minutes.

Using a food processor fitted with a metal blade, finely chop the mushrooms and onion.

Return the mixture to the saucepan and place over moderate heat. Add the flour and cook, stirring, until well blended. Gradually add the broth, whisking constantly to prevent lumps from forming. Simmer the soup over low heat for 20 minutes.

Add the lemon juice and parsley and simmer for 5 minutes more. Stir in the half-and-half and simmer, but do not boil. Season with salt and pepper to taste, and stir in the vermouth. Serve hot in warmed soup bowls.

Serves 8

MARY EMMERLING

Jalapeño Corn-Bread Muffins

1 cup yellow cornmeal
½ teaspoon salt
1 tablespoon baking powder
⅓ cup melted bacon fat or shortening
2 large eggs, beaten
1 cup cream-style canned corn
1 cup sour cream, or ⅔ cup buttermilk
1 medium onion, chopped
1 cup shredded sharp cheddar cheese
4 to 6 fresh or canned jalapeño peppers, or one 4-ounce
    can chopped green chilies, drained

Preheat the oven to 350°. Lightly oil a 12-cup muffin tin.

In a large bowl, combine the cornmeal, salt, and baking powder. Stir in the bacon fat. Add the eggs, creamed corn, and sour cream, and blend well. Stir in the onion.

Fill each muffin cup with 2 to 3 tablespoons of batter. Sprinkle on the cheese and chopped jalapeños, and top each with a smooth layer of the remaining batter.

Bake 35 to 40 minutes, or until a toothpick inserted in the center of a muffin comes out clean.

Allow the muffins to cool and remove from the cups.

Variation

If you think jalapeños are a bit too hot, substitute green chilies.

Makes 12 muffins.

MARY EMMERLING

A IDA Gabilondo is one of the premier cooks of Mexico and author of *Mexican Family Cooking*—and there's no better way to learn how to make authentic tortillas than from Aida.

♥ ♥   # Wheat-Flour Tortillas (Tortillas de Harina)

In the northern states of Mexico, tortillas are made with wheat flour. Corn flour is not used. Toasted in the oven, buttered, and sprinkled with grated cheese and a bit of ground red chile powder, flour tortillas make wonderful appetizers. A more elaborate version might include a pizza-style topping of green chile strips and cheese. Mouth-watering! Follow instructions to the letter, and there is no reason why you can't roll out a luscious, almost round flour tortilla.

Walnut-sized balls will result in beautiful miniature tortillas the size of a demitasse saucer. These are a delight folded in half and filled with crabmeat hash, or shredded pork, beef, or chicken (poached first), shredded mozzarella cheese and strips of green chile. A real treat that you'll never find on any restaurant menu!

> 6 cups all-purpose flour
> 1 teaspoon baking powder
> 2 teaspoons salt
> 1 heaping cup vegetable shortening
> 2 cups warm water, or a little more

Mix dry ingredients (not necessary to sift), work in shortening with hands until you get the consistency of oatmeal, then pour in the lukewarm water all at once. Mix well and knead for 2 to 3 minutes. Dough should be moist but manageable— a little drier than biscuit dough. Coat with a little oil or more soft shortening and put into a plastic bag for 20 minutes until dough is soft.

Take a large piece of dough and squeeze out a portion about the size of a Ping-Pong ball. Roll ball around in the palms of your hands until smooth. (It is best to prepare half the dough in balls while you keep remaining half in the plastic bag so it won't dry out.)

Using tips of fingers, flatten each ball slightly, then roll with a pin to the size of a saucer.

With griddle hot, cook the tortillas like flapjacks until they are cooked through and have developed brown spots. Do not scorch; lower heat as necessary to maintain an even temperature. The tortilla will puff up slightly as it cooks. Once you have turned a tortilla and completed the cooking cycle (both sides), press down with spatula about 30 seconds or more on all edges of the round so you produce a flat, golden disk, crisp and tasty. Do this on both sides.

Makes 36 regular-sized or 42 to 48 miniature-sized tortillas, depending on size of balls

AIDA GABILONDO

Reprinted by permission of Aida Gabilondo from *Mexican Family Cooking* by Aida Gabilondo. Copyright © 1986 by Ballantine Books.

W HEN Pope John Paul II visited the West Coast, all chefs in Los Angeles were vying to be the Pope's chef. **Ruggero Gadaldi** from CARDINI RESTAURANT in the Los Angeles Hilton was given that honor. So we invited him to bring us the exact recipes from one of the Pope's meals. The two recipes that follow were designed for His Eminence. Why not try them for your families?

♥ ## Roasted Veal Rack with Morel Mushroom Sauce

One 4-to 4¼-pound veal rack
1 shallot
2 ounces dry morel mushrooms
1 shot of brandy
½ cup dry white wine
2 cups heavy cream
6 sprigs fresh rosemary
Salt and pepper

In a roasting pan, sear the meat that is already tied. Put it in a 400° oven for 20 minutes. Remove the meat from the pan and keep it warm. Discard the grease and in the same pan sauté the shallot (finely chopped) and mushrooms (soaked and washed in water). Deglaze with brandy and white wine. Reduce by ⅓ and add cream and rosemary. Salt and pepper to taste. To serve, slice the meat in 6 portions, add sauce on the top, and garnish with rosemary sprigs.

Serves 8

RUGGERO GADALDI

♥ ♥ **Capri Salad**

Salad Lettuces

6 bunches mâche (or corn salad)
6 bunches baby red oak leaf lettuce
1 head curly endive
1 small head radicchio
1 small head Boston lettuce
2 bunches arugula

Salad Ingredients

½ pound fresh-made bocconcini mozzarella
2 ounces sun-dried tomatoes marinated in olive oil
12 cherry tomatoes
12 baby pear yellow tomatoes
½ -ounce bunch fresh oregano
1 ounce black olives

Sauce

1 shallot, finely chopped
10 leaves fresh basil, finely chopped
6 tablespoons extra-virgin olive oil
4 tablespoons balsamic vinegar

Wash salad lettuces and dry. Tear each leaf individually into small pieces and put into a salad bowl.

In another bowl start to prepare salad ingredients. Julienne the sun-dried tomatoes; cut in half the cherry and pear tomatoes, and slice the mozzarella. Add the fresh oregano and black olives.

Put the sauce ingredients in an 8-ounce jar and shake it for a couple of seconds. Add salt and white pepper to taste. Mix half of the sauce with lettuce and put the other half of the sauce in mozzarella, tomatoes, and other ingredients.

Place the lettuces in the middle of the plate. Elegantly arrange the mozzarella and tomatoes on top.

Serves 6 to 8

RUGGERO GADALDI

NIKKI and **David Goldbeck** are authors of several cookbooks. The brownie and baked alaska recipes happen to come from their book called *American Wholefoods Cuisine,* which contains recipes for delicious, wholesome, additive-free meatless meals. And the Goldbecks always create recipes with another important detail in mind—how you can make a great meal without having to spend a lot of time in the kitchen. Who wouldn't appreciate that?

 ## Baked Fruits Alaska

An elegant low-calorie dessert.

> 1 cantaloupe
> Fresh peaches, cut up (enough peaches and berries to fill hollowed cantaloupe halves)
> Berries of your choice
> 1 egg white
> ½ teaspoon honey
> ⅛ teaspoon vanilla extract

Preheat oven to 450°.

Cut cantaloupe in half and scoop out seeds. If melon is small, cut in half crosswise rather than from end to end to make a deeper hollow. Cut a thin slice from rounded ends so melon halves sit comfortably. Fill cavity with peaches and berries.

Beat egg white until stiff. Fold in honey and vanilla. Spread over cantaloupe halves to completely seal the fruit within the mountain of meringue.

Bake for 5 to 8 minutes until golden. Serve at once.

Serves 2

NIKKI AND DAVID GOLDBECK

Nikki's New Brownies

Our well-loved brownie recipe is even better now with combined unrefined sweeteners.

    3 squares (3 ounces) unsweetened baking chocolate
    6 tablespoons milk
    3 eggs
    ¾ cup honey
    ⅓ cup maple syrup
    1½ teaspoons vanilla extract
    ½ teaspoon salt
    1 cup whole wheat flour
    ¼ cup oil
    ¾ cup walnut pieces

Preheat oven to 350°.

Combine chocolate and milk in a small saucepan or the top of a double boiler and cook over very low heat or a flame tamer until chocolate is creamy. Remove from heat and let cool a little.

Beat eggs with honey, maple syrup, and vanilla. Beat in cooled chocolate and remaining ingredients. Pour into an oiled 9 × 13-inch baking pan.

Bake for 25 minutes. Cool in the pan and cut into squares to serve.

Makes 18 brownies

NIKKI AND DAVID GOLDBECK

Reprinted by permission of Nikki and David Goldbeck from *American Wholefoods Cuisine* by David and Nikki Goldbeck. Copyright © 1983 by New American Library.

Warm Chef's Salad

 1 teaspoon unsalted butter
 1 large green onion, bulb and green top, minced
 1 clove garlic, minced
 2 teaspoons Dijon mustard
 1 tablespoon red wine vinegar
 1 teaspoon lemon juice
 6 teaspoons olive oil
 1 teaspoon vodka
 ½ pound wax beans, trimmed, cut French style, blanched 3
    minutes
 1 small red bell pepper, seeded, cut into strips, blanched 3
    minutes
 ¼ pound thinly sliced cooked smoked ham, cut into strips
 1 teaspoon chopped fresh basil
 1 head of lettuce
 ½ cups roughly chopped fresh parsley

Melt butter in skillet over medium heat. Add green onion; cook 1 minute.
Add garlic; cook 3 minutes. Mix mustard, vinegar, and lemon juice in a small
bowl. Slowly add oil and vodka. Add the wax beans to the skillet, along with

the bell pepper, ham, and basil. Cook, tossing constantly, until warmed through. Toss in lettuce. Pour vinaigrette over the top and toss once more. Sprinkle with parsley. Serve immediately.

Serves 4

BERT GREENE

♥ ## Broiled Fruits with Peach Cream

    ½ pineapple, peeled, cored, cut into ½-inch-thick slices,
        then quartered
     2 large persimmons, each cut into 8 strips
     1 small cantaloupe, cut into balls
  8–10 large strawberries
     2 tablespoons dark brown sugar, sifted
    ½ cup sour cream
    ½ cup DeKuyper's Peachtree Schnapps
     3 tablespoons orange juice

Arrange the fruit on a large, shallow heatproof platter, starting with pineapple and alternating with rows of persimmon strips, melon balls, and strawberries. Dust the fruit with the sifted brown sugar.

In a small bowl, combine the sour cream, Peachtree Schnapps, and orange juice. Whisk until smooth. Chill.

Place the arranged fruit under a preheated broiler until the sugar has melted into the fruit (4 to 5 minutes). Serve warm or well chilled with the Peach Cream.

Serves 6 to 8

BERT GREENE

> **B**ORN in Germany, **Dieter Hannig** began his training as a kitchen apprentice at the age of thirteen. Since then he's worked as sous-chef for the Grand Hotel in Leysin and the Eurotel St. Moritz in Switzerland. And he began his career with Hilton International in November 1974. He made a sea bass from his cookbook—the fish was low in calories and low in salt, tasted wonderful, and looked elegant too! *Dining in Grand Style*—that certainly lived up to its title!

♥ ♥　　　　　## Baked Sea Bass with Caraway

When Kazuhito Endo was sous-chef of the Vista International in New York, he created this simple and attractive dish, and a number of other low-calorie, low-sodium main courses for the changing menus, which regularly feature light, health-wise specials.

Slivers of Belgian endive and tomato, dressed with a light curry vinaigrette touched with tarragon, form an unusual backdrop for the caraway-topped sea bass fillets, decorated with their natural motif of black netting. Surprisingly big flavor and satisfying texture make this dish a success with dieters—as well as other customers. If you prefer salt, add to taste—but the natural bitter-sweetness of the endive and the punch of curry and caraway will be sufficient seasoning for most.

½ teaspoon curry powder
¼ cup tarragon vinegar
½ cup light vegetable oil
   Lemon juice
   Four 5-ounce sea bass fillets with skin (for this you'll
      need two bass, each weighing 1¼–1½ pounds)
2 teaspoons caraway seeds
1 pound small Belgian endives, halved, cored, and cut
      crosswise into thin slices
1 medium tomato, peeled, seeded, and cut into thin strips
   Fresh tarragon leaves or chervil sprigs

Preheat the broiler. Blend together the curry powder and vinegar in a small bowl. Beat in the oil gradually, then add lemon juice to taste.

Place the fillets, flesh side down, on an oiled broiler pan. Score the skin diagonally every 1½ inches or so. Sprinkle with the caraway. Set the pan under the broiler at the middle level. Cook for about 5 minutes, until just opaque throughout.

Meanwhile, toss together the endive, tomato, and tarragon leaves with the dressing. Arrange on 4 serving plates.

Arrange a fillet on each salad; serve at once. *(This dish should be served as soon as the fish emerges from the broiler to enjoy the contrast of the juicy-firm hot sea bass and the cool, crisp salad.)*

Serves 4

DIETER HANNIG

Reprinted by permission of Dieter Hannig from *Dining in Grand Style* by Dieter Hannig. Copyright © 1988 by Thorsons Publishers, Inc.

WOULDN'T it be great to be able to cook a meal from your favorite restaurant in your *own* kitchen? **Natalie Haughton** does just that. She's the food editor of *The Daily News* in the San Fernando Valley of Los Angeles and she brought along a recipe for Barbecued Chicken Pizza. This has become a popular recipe in the gourmet pizza restaurants cropping up across the country.

♥ ♥   ## Barbecued Chicken Pizza

Pizza dough for 12"–14" pizza pan (purchase dough at Italian deli or prepare homemade)
1 cup barbecue sauce
3 to 4 thin slices red onion, cut in half and separated into pieces
2 cups cut-up barbecued chicken (breast and legs from 1¼-pound chicken or 1 to 1¼ pounds chicken breasts)
3 cups grated smoked Gouda cheese
2 to 3 tablespoons chopped fresh cilantro

Stretch pizza dough to fit into lightly greased 14-inch pizza pan. Spread barbecue sauce evenly over top of pizza dough just to the edges. Sprinkle evenly with onion pieces, chicken, grated cheese as desired, and cilantro.

Bake in preheated 500° oven (on top shelf) for 15 minutes, or until crust is golden brown. Serve immediately.

Makes 8 to 10 wedges

NATALIE HAUGHTON

WHO doesn't like chocolate? And if you're among the few who doesn't, you may be turned around by one of the recipes from **Janice Wald Henderson,** author of *The White Chocolate Cookbook.* Here are two of the most delicious-tasting, elegant-looking desserts to be consumed!

Riesling-Poached Pears with White Chocolate Ganache

The pears are delicately poached in Riseling and then coated with a smooth white chocolate ganache. It's an easy, elegant fruit dessert that's also visually appealing. The creator, Greg Higgins, is executive chef at the Heathman Hotel in Portland, Oregon.

Pears

1 bottle Riesling wine (750 milliliters)
2 cups sugar
4 whole cloves
2 bay leaves
1 vanilla bean
6 whole ripe Bartlett pears

Ganache

1 cup heavy (whipping) cream
10 ounces white chocolate, finely chopped

Garnish

6 mint sprigs

Poach the pears: In a large heavy saucepan over medium heat, bring the Riseling to a simmer with the sugar, cloves, bay leaves, and vanilla bean.

Using a sharp knife, peel the pears as smoothly as possible, leaving the stems on. Remove the entire core from the bottom side of the pears. Lower the pears into the simmering syrup (reduce the heat to low, if necessary) and poach until they are tender, about 20 minutes. Remove the pears from the liquid and set aside to cool.

Strain the poaching liquid through a fine-mesh strainer and return to the saucepan. Boil over high heat until the syrup reaches 238° on a candy thermometer. Cool completely. Set aside.

Make the ganache: In a saucepan over medium-high heat, bring the cream to a boil and remove from heat. Gradually whisk in the white chocolate until the mixture is smooth.

Assemble: Pat the pears dry with paper towels and cut a small portion off the bottom of each pear so it will stand upright. Place the pears upright in a shallow dish or pan and carefully ladle the ganache over each to achieve a smooth coating. Remove to a serving plate and carefully coat again to achieve an even coating. A small amount of ganache will rest in a circle around each pear. Allow the pears to cool completely.

Place each pear on a dessert plate, spoon some of the poaching syrup around it, and garnish with a mint sprig.

Serves 6

JANICE WALD HENDERSON

Blonde Bombshell

Shaped like a classic bombe, this dessert features a skinny layer of white chocolate cake which encases a delicate, rum-flavored white chocolate mousse. Frankly, this bombshell is a knockout. Samantha Fox, who created it, is a Los Angeles–based caterer and food writer.

Shell

1/4 pound unsalted butter
9 ounces white chocolate, finely chopped
2 large eggs, at room temperature
1/2 cup sugar
1 teaspoon vanilla extract
1 cup flour

Filling

6 tablespoons unsalted butter
6 ounces white chocolate, finely chopped
4 large eggs, separated, at room temperature
3/4 cup sugar
1/4 cup rum
1 envelope unflavored gelatin

1½ cups heavy (whipping) cream, whipped to soft peaks
3 tablespoons confectioners' sugar

Make the shell: Position a rack in the center and preheat oven to 350°. Lightly butter the bottom and sides of an 11 × 17-inch jelly-roll pan. Line the pan with parchment paper so that the paper overhangs each end by about 1 inch. Dust the pan with flour; tap out the excess. In a heavy medium-sized saucepan over low heat, melt the butter. Remove the saucepan from the heat, add the white chocolate, and stir until the white chocolate is melted and smooth.

Using an electric mixer set at medium speed, beat the eggs and the sugar in a medium bowl until thick and light. Beat in the white chocolate mixture and vanilla until well blended. Add the flour and stir until combined. Using a rubber spatula, spread the batter evenly into the prepared pan. The layer will be very thin. Bake until a cake tester inserted in the center comes out clean, about 20 minutes. Transfer the cake in the pan to a wire rack and let cool for 10 minutes, then invert the cake onto a clean, flat surface and carefully peel off the paper.

Line a 6-cup glass bowl with enough plastic wrap to overhang the edges by at least 1 inch. Measure the diameter of the bottom of the bowl and cut out a same-size circle of the cake, working from one corner of the cake. Fit it into the bottom of the bowl. Measure the circumference and depth of the bowl and cut out a rectangle of cake of that proportion. Fit it into the bowl, starting at the base of the cake and wrapping it around the sides. (The cake is very flexible and will not tear.) If necessary, patch any holes with cake pieces cut to size. Save any large cake pieces to cover the bombe. Place the small scraps and hard edges into a food processor fitted with a metal blade and process, using on-off pulses, until contents resemble fine crumbs. Set aside 1 cup of crumbs.

Make the filling: In a heavy medium-sized saucepan over low heat, melt the butter. Remove the saucepan from the heat, add the white chocolate, and stir until melted and smooth.

Using an electric mixer set at medium speed, beat the egg yolks and sugar in a large bowl until a thick ribbon forms when beaters are lifted. Beat in the white chocolate mixture until well blended. Pour the rum into a heatproof cup, then add the gelatin and let it soften. Place the cup in a pan of barely simmering water, stirring until the gelatin dissolves, about 1 minute, then add to the white chocolate mixture, mixing well. Fold in the reserved cup of crumbs. Fold half of the whipped cream into the white chocolate mixture to lighten it, then fold in the remaining cream.

Using an electric mixer set at low speed, beat the egg whites in a grease-free small bowl until they start to foam. Gradually increase the speed to high and continue beating until the egg whites form stiff peaks. Fold ¼ of the beaten egg whites into the mousse to lighten it, then fold in the remaining egg whites. Spoon the filling into the prepared mold, cover with leftover pieces of cake, and refrigerate until completely set, at least 4 hours.

Assemble: Invert the bombe onto a large serving platter and carefully peel off the plastic wrap. Sift the confectioners' sugar over the top of the bombe. Untwist a wire hanger and straighten it. Heat a 6-inch strip of the hanger over a gas flame until it is red-hot. Starting at one end of the sugar-coated top, use this makeshift "branding iron" to caramelize a straight line down the center and down the other side of the bombe. You may have to reheat the hanger periodically. Repeat the process by caramelizing another line across the center of the cake at a right angle to the first. Burn in two more lines so that they form a pattern of eight equal wedges. Cut the cake with a sharp knife, using a sawing motion.

Do ahead: The bombe can be made and refrigerated up to 2 days in advance.

Serves 16

JANICE WALD HENDERSON

Reprinted by permission of Janice Wald Henderson from *The White Chocolate Cookbook*. Copyright © 1987 by Janice Wald Henderson, Contemporary Books.

S HARON Tyler Herbst, who we sometimes refer to as the "bread lady," brought us two recipes from her latest cookbook, *Simply Sensational Desserts*. Either of them will satisfy your sweet tooth.

Coconut Shortbread

1¾ cups all-purpose flour
½ teaspoon baking powder
¼ teaspoon salt
¾ cup butter, softened
⅓ cup granulated sugar
1½ teaspoons vanilla extract
1 cup flaked coconut
6 ounces semisweet chocolate, melted with 2 teaspoons vegetable oil

In a medium bowl, combine flour, baking powder, and salt; set aside. In a small mixing bowl, beat butter, sugar, and vanilla together until light and fluffy. Stir in flour mixture ½ cup at a time, blending well after each addition. Stir in coconut. Form dough into a 4 × 7-inch rectangle. Wrap and freeze or refrigerate until firm, 1 to 4 hours.

Preheat oven to 300°. Grease 2 large baking sheets. On a floured surface, roll dough out into an 8 × 14-inch rectangle about ¼ inch thick. Using a floured knife with a long blade, cut dough in 28 (2-inch) squares, cutting 4 strips one way and 7 strips the other way. Arrange squares, 1 inch apart, on prepared baking sheets.

Bake 25 to 30 minutes, or until golden. Cool on racks.

Line 2 large baking sheets with waxed paper; set aside. Turn melted chocolate mixture into a small deep bowl. Dip half of each cookie diagonally into chocolate, shaking off excess. Arrange on prepared baking sheets. Refrigerate until chocolate sets, about 10 minutes.

Store in an airtight container at room temperature 1 week; freeze for longer storage.

Makes 28 cookies

SHARON TYLER HERBST

Reprinted by permission of Sharon Tyler Herbst from *The Joy of Cookies*. Copyright © 1987 by Barron's Educational Series, Inc.

Cookie Monsters

1 cup butter, softened
1 cup brown sugar, packed
½ cup granulated sugar
2 eggs
1½ teaspoons vanilla extract
1 teaspoon ground cinnamon
½ teaspoon ground nutmeg
½ teaspoon salt
1½ cups all-purpose flour
1 teaspoon baking soda
2 cups rolled oats, regular or quick-cooking
1 cup shredded or flaked coconut
About 1¼ cups multicolored plain or peanut
candy-covered chocolate pieces, raisins,
chocolate-covered raisins, semisweet chocolate pieces,
malted milk balls, chopped nuts, gum drops, jelly beans,
or candy corn

Preheat oven to 350°. Generously grease 5 round 8-inch foil or regular pie pans. Place a round of waxed paper on bottom of each pie pan; grease waxed paper. In a large mixing bowl, beat butter and sugars until light and fluffy. Add eggs, vanilla, cinnamon, nutmeg, and salt; beat until blended. Stir in flour, baking soda, oats, and coconut. Divide dough evenly between prepared pans. With the back of a large spoon, spread dough evenly over bottom of pans. Sprinkle about ¼ cup of your favorite topping over each cookie. If desired, write a name or message with connecting pieces of chosen topping. Bake 15 to 20 minutes or until browned. Cool in pans. Turn cooled cookies out of pans; remove waxed-paper rounds. To serve, cut each cookie into 8 wedges. Makes 5 giant cookies (40 pieces).

Variation

Chocolate-Raisin Drop Cookies: Stir ½ cup semisweet chocolate pieces and ½ cup raisins into dough. Drop by rounded teaspoons 1½ inches apart on greased baking sheets. Bake in a preheated 375° oven 8 to 10 minutes, or until golden brown. Let stand 3 minutes before carefully removing from baking sheets. Cool on racks.

Tip: Cut gumdrops, dates, marshmallows, candied fruits, and other sticky foods with scissors. Dip scissors into hot water occasionally to make cutting easier.

Makes about 72 two-inch cookies.

SHARON TYLER HERBST

M ABEL Hoffman, who has written several bestselling cookbooks, brought along a recipe from her newest cookbook, *Make Ahead Entertaining*. Naturally, the concept allows you to enjoy your party along with your guests if everything's prepared in advance. Holiday Vegetable Tidbits are colorful red and green appetizers that are as nutritious as they are delicious. They can be enjoyed at any time of the year, so don't let the name of the recipe influence you.

Holiday Vegetable Tidbits

One 4-ounce package blue cheese or Roquefort cheese
One 3-ounce package cream cheese, room temperature
½ teaspoon Worcestershire sauce
2 teaspoons minced fresh chives or green onion
⅛ teaspoon salt
⅛ teaspoon pepper
3 tablespoons dairy sour cream
½ teaspoon Dijon-style mustard

16 cherry tomatoes
Chopped green onion or parsley
1 large zucchini
Pimento strips

In a small bowl or a food processor fitted with a metal blade, beat or process blue or Roquefort cheese, cream cheese, Worcestershire sauce, minced chives or green onions, salt, pepper, sour cream, and mustard until blended. *Complete now or make ahead.*

To complete now, cut off tops of cherry tomatoes. Scoop out centers. Invert tomato shells on paper towels and drain 15 to 20 minutes. Spoon about 1½ teaspoons cheese mixture into each drained tomato. Garnish tops with chopped green onions or parsley. Cut zucchini into 16 crosswise slices; mound 1 level teaspoon cheese mixture on each zucchini slice. Garnish slices with a pimento strip. Serve on platter or serving plate.

To make ahead, prepare cheese mixture 2 to 3 days ahead. Spoon into container with a tight-fitting lid; refrigerate. About 3½ hours before serving, prepare vegetables. Fill or top vegetables with cheese mixture; refrigerate up to 3 hours. Garnish and serve as directed above.

Makes 32 appetizer tidbits

MABEL HOFFMAN

RAIMUND Hofmeister has been the chef at the Century Plaza Hotel in Los Angeles for the past eight years. And if you've ever dined there, you'll know why their guests return year after year. One couple who has dined there through the years is the President and Mrs. Reagan. Chef Hofmeister joined us to cook us the same meal the Reagans were served in 1984. And he told me he had a cookbook "in the making." If the recipes are all like this one, I'm anxious to get a copy!

Suprême of Capon with Celery and Mushrooms in Tarragon-Flavored Lemon Sauce

Stuffing

1 tablespoon butter
½ teaspoon garlic, crushed with salt

1 tablespoon finely diced shallots
½ cup finely diced celery
¾ cup diced mushrooms
Dash white wine
Juice of ½ lemon
2 tablespoons breadcrumbs
1 egg yolk
1 tablespoon rough-chopped parsley
1 teaspoon rough-chopped tarragon
Salt and pepper
Eight 8-ounce single capon breasts
1 tablespoon diced shallots
2 cups chicken stock
½ cup California Chardonnay
2 lemons each for juice and zest
1 cup reduced cream
3 tablespoons butter

Make stuffing: Preheat pan, add 1 tablespoon butter, garlic, shallots, and celery and sauté 2 to 3 minutes. Add mushrooms, dash of white wine, and juice of ½ lemon; sauté until liquid evaporates. Mix in breadcrumbs, egg yolk, parsley, and tarragon; add salt and pepper to taste. Set aside to cool.

Meantime, remove skin from capon breasts, clean wing bones, and chop off the tip joints. Split capon breasts from thick part to create a pocketlike cut. Fill in stuffing, equally distributed; fold meat back together. Spice with salt and pepper. Brown off breast on both sides and set them in butter-greased shallow pan sprinkled with shallots. Add chicken stock and Chardonnay, cover with parchment paper, and put in 375° oven approximately 12 to 15 minutes.

Take breasts out of pan and place them on serving platter, 4 left, 4 right. Pour left over liquid through fine strainer into smaller pan, add lemon juice and zest, and boil up for a minute; add cream. Monte with fresh butter and nappe the supremes.

Note: This recipe was served to the President of the United States, Mr. Ronald W. Reagan, and First Lady on December 27, 1984, at the new tower suite of the Century Plaza Hotel, for a quiet dinner for two.

Serves 6 to 8

RAIMUND HOFMEISTER

♥ ♥   Shredded Chicken with Sesame Seeds

Ingredients

½ pound boneless chicken breasts, skinned
1 egg white
½ teaspoon salt
2 teaspoons cornstarch
⅔ cup oil, preferably peanut
1 tablespoon white sesame seeds, untoasted

Sauce

1 teaspoon dark soy sauce
1 teaspoon Chinese black rice vinegar or cider vinegar
½ teaspoon chili bean sauce
1 teaspoon sugar
½ teaspoon roasted Sichuan peppercorns
2 teaspoons finely chopped scallions
½ teaspoon sesame oil
2 teaspoons rice wine or dry sherry

Cut the chicken breasts into fine shreds 3 inches long. Combine them with the egg white, salt, and cornstarch; chill about 20 minutes.

Heat the oil in a wok or large skillet until moderately hot. Add chicken mixture and stir-fry quickly in oil to keep from sticking. Cook until it turns white, about 1 minute. Drain chicken immediately in a colander or sieve and drain off oil.

Clean the wok and add about 1 tablespoon of the drained oil. Reheat until hot. Add sesame seeds and stir-fry them 1 minute, or until they are slightly brown. Then add the sauce ingredients and bring to a boil. Return the cooked chicken to pan and stir-fry mixture for another 2 minutes, coating the pieces thoroughly with the sauce and sesame seeds. Serve at once, or let it cool and serve at room temperature.

Serves 2

KEN HOM

♥ ♥   Lettuce with Oyster Sauce

Here is lettuce prepared in a very familiar Chinese way—blanched and served with oyster sauce. Lettuce prepared like this retains a crispy texture and its delicate flavor is unimpaired by cooking. The combination makes a simple, quickly prepared, tasty vegetable dish.

    1 head romaine or iceberg lettuce (about 1½ pounds)
    3 tablespoons oyster sauce
    1 tablespoon oil

Separate the lettuce leaves and blanch them in a pot of boiling salted water for about 30 seconds, or until they have wilted slightly.

Remove them and drain well. Mix the oyster sauce with the oil.

Arrange the lettuce leaves on a serving dish, pour the oyster sauce mixture over it, and serve immediately.

Serves 4 to 6

KEN HOM

YOU don't have to be English to love scones—and in fact, **Angela Hynes** tells me you don't have to be English to *make* scones. Here are two recipes that will lead you through step by step to an English treat. They're both in Angela's book called *The Pleasures of Afternoon Tea*.

Oven Scones

This basic oven scone is what's used for the famous "cream tea." Serve the scones fresh and warm from the oven accompanied by a pot of jam—preferably straw-berry—and a dish of cream. Ideally, the cream should be clotted cream, that particularly rich variety that comes from Devonshire in England. English cream is difficult to get in the United States, but a few specialty stores do import it so check your local gourmet emporia. Failing that, serve a dish of unsweetened whipped cream. To eat, split your scone, generously spread each piece with jam, and top with a spoonful of cream.

2 cups self-rising flour
1 tablespoon baking powder
Pinch of salt
2 tablespoons cold butter, cut in small pieces
1–1⅓ cups milk, plus a little more for brushing on scones
Butter

. Preheat oven to 450°. Very lightly grease a large baking sheet; set aside. Sift flour, baking powder, and salt into a large bowl. With your fingers, rub in cold butter until mixture is crumbly. Make a well in center of mixture; add milk and mix with a fork to make a dough that *barely* holds together (you may need to press dough together with your hands).

Turn out onto a floured surface and knead lightly just until smooth. Roll out with a floured rolling pin or pat dough with your hands to make a round about ¾ inch thick. Cut in rounds with a 2-inch fluted or plain cookie cutter. Arrange 1 to 1½ inches apart on baking sheet; brush tops lightly with milk.

Bake 8 to 10 minutes, or until well risen and golden. Transfer to a wire rack and cool 5 minutes. Split and serve warm with butter.

Variation

Rich Oven Scones—Add 1 tablespoon sugar to the dry ingredients. In place of the ⅔ cup milk, use a mixture of 1 lightly beaten egg and 5 tablespoons milk.

Makes about 12 scones

ANGELA HYNES

Caribbean Scones

West Indians living in England have created this deliciously exotic adaptation of the good old scone.

1 cup all-purpose flour
2 teaspoons baking powder
½ teaspoon salt
1 teaspoon sugar
1 cup mashed, cooked sweet potatoes
3 tablespoons butter, melted and cooled
Butter
Honey, if desired

Preheat oven to 375°. Grease a baking sheet; set aside. Sift flour, baking powder, and salt into a medium-sized bowl; stir in sugar. In a large bowl, thoroughly mix potatoes and 1½ tablespoons melted butter with a fork. Add dry ingredients and mix to form a soft dough.

Turn out onto a floured surface. Roll out with a floured rolling pin or pat dough with your hands to make a round about ½ inch thick. Cut in rounds with a 2-inch fluted or plain cookie cutter. Place 1 to 1½ inches apart on baking sheet; brush tops with remaining 1½ tablespoons melted butter.

Bake about 20 minutes or until light brown. Split and serve warm with butter and honey.

Makes about 10 scones

ANGELA HYNES

Reprinted by permission of Angela Hynes from *The Pleasures of Afternoon Tea* by Angela Hynes copyright © 1987 by HP Books.

DAVID Keh has been cooking Chinese food professionally since the age of fourteen. He is said to have introduced Szechuan cooking to the United States and he is one of the most successful restaurant entrepreneurs in New York City. Currently he owns and personally manages four Chinese restaurants in Manhattan (PIG HEAVEN, AUNTIE YUAN'S, DAVID K'S RESTAURANT, and DAVID K'S CAFÉ). Each restaurant has its own specialties and its own cuisine. DAVID K'S RESTAURANT specializes in low-cholesterol, low-fat, low-salt, and MSG-free foods. The two recipes that follow are terrific meals. (David was very close to the late Danny Kaye who, besides being a great comedian, happened to be one of the most accomplished Chinese chefs. And when he went to David's restaurant he would spend his time cooking and trading recipes with chefs in the kitchen.)

♥ ## Quick Sautéed Prawns

Oil
10–12 prawns mixed with ½ teaspoon wine, ½ teaspoons
cornstarch, and ½ egg white
½ clove garlic, sliced
½ cup sliced onion
⅓ cup sliced scallions

½ cup shredded green bell pepper
⅓ cup shredded red bell pepper
1 thinly shredded ginger root
Salt and pepper
Sugar
½ cup coriander

Heat 2 cups oil in a wok over high heat. Fry the prawns about 2 minutes; drain and set aside. Heat 2 tablespoons oil in the wok. Brown garlic slices slightly, then add all vegetables and ginger root (add harder-to-cook vegetables first). Stir-fry about 3 minutes. Mix the cooked prawns with the vegetables. Add salt, pepper, and sugar to taste. Place coriander on top and serve with brown rice.

Serves 4

DAVID KEH

Danny Kaye's Shredded Vegetables with Chinese Sausage and Whole Wheat Pancakes

Oil
1 stick sausage, shredded
½ cup shredded carrots
½ cup shredded garlic shoots
1 cup shredded cabbage
1 cup soaked shining noodles
Whole Wheat Pancakes (recipe follows)

Heat 2 tablespoons oil in a wok. Stir-fry sausage 1½ minutes; drain and set aside. Heat 2 tablespoons oil. Add the vegetables; stir-fry 2 minutes. Add pre-cooked sausage to wok, then shining noodles. Toss and serve with whole wheat pancakes.

Whole Wheat Pancakes

1 cup whole wheat flour
1 cup all-purpose flour
1 cup boiling water

Combine the flours in a bowl. Pour in the hot water; mix and knead until dough is smooth. Rest the dough at least 15 minutes. Divide into 12 pieces. Roll out each piece to a thin circular shape. Place pancakes in a flat pan one at a time and cook on low heat 1 minute on each side.

Makes 12 servings

DAVID KEH

ESTIMATES indicate that this year alone 11 million microwaves will be sold. And if you're like me, you do little more than bake potatoes and heat up a cup of coffee in your microwave. It's no wonder **Margie Kreschollek,** author of *The Guaranteed Goof Proof Microwave Cookbook,* says that very few people use a microwave to its fullest advantage. Here are two recipes that taste great and take less than an hour, start to finish!

♥ ## Stuffed Fish Roll-Ups

For those of you who like your fillets stuffed, have I got a recipe for you! You can just poach these fillets in wine and serve them plain, or you can try my lovely Lemon Sauce (recipe follows), which adds a finishing touch for a perfect presentation.

    2 tablespoons butter
    2 cloves garlic, minced
 ½ cup chopped celery
 ¼ cup chopped fresh mushrooms
 ½ cup chopped onion
    4 ounces fresh small or medium-sized shrimp, chopped
1 ½ cups flavored breadcrumbs
    1 tablespoon fresh lemon juice
 ½ teaspoon seasoned salt
 ⅛ teaspoon pepper
    1 egg, slightly beaten

Eight 2-ounce fish fillets of your choice (sole and
flounder work well)
¼ cup white wine

Place butter, garlic, celery, mushrooms, onion, and shrimp in a 1-quart bowl. Microwave on HIGH for 3 minutes. Stir; microwave on HIGH another 3 minutes. Stir in breadcrumbs, lemon juice, seasoned salt, pepper, and egg. Mix lightly but well. Place 1 heaping tablespoon of crumb mixture on the center of each fillet. Bring fish ends over stuffing, pushing gently into stuffing to hold.

In a round glass baking dish or pie plate, arrange fish pointing toward the center of the dish in a wheel-spoke design. Add wine, cover with wax paper, and elevate flat-bottomed dish on an inverted saucer. Place on a turntable if available. Microwave on HIGH for 7 minutes. (If not using turntable, microwave for 3 minutes on HIGH, then rotate ¼ turn, microwave for another 3 minutes on HIGH, rotating dish another ¼ turn, and microwave 1 final minute on HIGH until fish flakes easily with a fork.)

Variations

Try adding clams, lobster, or crabmeat to the stuffing in place of the shrimp or in addition to it.

Serves 4 to 5

MARGIE KRESCHOLLEK

Lemon Sauce

2 tablespoons butter
¼ cup chopped scallions
1 tablespoon cornstarch
1 cup chicken broth
2 teaspoons fresh lemon juice
¼ teaspoon grated lemon zest

Place butter and scallions in a 2-cup glass measure and microwave on HIGH for 1 minute. Whisk and microwave on HIGH for 2 minutes more. Add cornstarch and broth. Whisk until smooth and microwave on HIGH for 4 minutes, whisking each minute.

Stir in lemon juice and zest. Microwave 1 minute more on HIGH and serve over fish rolls.

Makes 1¼ cups

MARGIE KRESCHOLLEK

♥ ♥　　**Rocking Horse Ranch Texas Chili**

This recipe, which comes from a Catskills dude ranch, has a wonderful way with spices that I know you lovers of "hot stuff" will enjoy. On the other hand, if you love only slightly warm things, tone down the amount of spices you use and taste as you add them. The key is taste, taste, taste—and keep in mind my motto: Skinny cooks can't be trusted!

This recipe freezes beautifully. For easy defrosting, line the container you will use to reheat in with plastic wrap. Ladle in the chili and freeze. Once frozen, remove the block from the container, wrap in freezer wrap, then label with contents, date, and the container it was frozen in. When you're ready to defrost and heat, just unwrap the block, pop it into the appropriate container, and you're ready to go.

>   2 pounds hamburger
>   2 cloves garlic, minced
>   2 medium onions, diced
>   1 green pepper, diced
>   1 cup sliced fresh mushrooms or one 8-ounce can sliced mushrooms, drained
>   Two 16-ounce cans red kidney beans, drained and rinsed
> 5–8 tablespoons chili powder
>   ¼ teaspoon crushed red pepper
>   ⅛ teaspoon oregano
>   ⅛ teaspoon basil
>   1 teaspoon Tabasco sauce
>   ¼ teaspoon salt
>   ⅛ teaspoon pepper
>   2 medium fresh tomatoes, peeled and diced into small chunks
>   One 28-ounce can peeled and crushed tomatoes
>   Dash of thyme

Crumble hamburger into a colander set into a casserole dish. Microwave on HIGH for 3 minutes. Break up meat with a fork and add garlic, onions, and green pepper.

Microwave on HIGH for another 3 minutes, break up meat, and discard fat.

In a 3- or 4-quart deep casserole dish, combine meat, mushrooms, drained kidney beans, and spices to taste, mixing together well. Add fresh and canned tomatoes and thyme, and cover with vented plastic wrap. If using a flat-bottomed container, elevate on an inverted saucer—it would help to use a turntable if available.

Microwave on HIGH for 5 minutes, remove the plastic wrap, and continue microwaving on 50 percent power or MEDIUM for 35 to 45 minutes, until slightly thickened and flavors blend, stirring several times. (If not using a turntable, rotate dish ¼ turn each time you stir.)

Let stand, covered, for 5 minutes before serving. Dish into bowls, or serve with large corn chips for an appetizer.

Tips: If you use a square-cornered container you may find that whatever sets in the corners will be dried out, so stir frequently.
If you don't have fresh tomatoes, substitute whole canned tomatoes.

Serves 4 to 6

MARGIE KRESCHOLLEK

S HEILA Lukins, half of the team that wrote *The Silver Palate Cook-book* and *The Silver Palate Good Times Cookbook,* visited *Hour's* kitchen. Both Sheila and **Julee Russo,** owners of THE SILVER PALATE in New York City, have created recipes for cooking and entertaining during every season of the year. They even quote Virginia Woolf who said, "One cannot think well, love well, sleep well, if one has not dined well." Here are two Silver Palate recipes that will help you and your guests dine well!

♥  **Herbed Asparagus**

2 pounds fresh asparagus, tough ends removed
4 tablespoons unsalted butter, at room temperature
1 tablespoon chopped Italian parsley
1 tablespoon chopped fresh or freeze-dried chives
1 tablespoon chopped fresh dill
1 tablespoon chopped fresh rosemary

1 teaspoon butcher grind black pepper
¼- pound wedge fresh Parmesan cheese

Blanch asparagus in boiling water for 1½ to 2 minutes, or until just tender. Remove to paper towel and pat dry. In a small bowl, combine butter with chopped herbs and pepper.

Just before serving, melt butter over medium heat in a large heavy skillet. Add asparagus and toss gently. Remove to a serving platter and shave Parmesan cheese over asparagus. Serve immediately.

Serves 6

SHEILA LUKINS

Chocolate Mousse

We love our Silver Palate chocolate mousse recipe so much that it's hard to think of changing the basic combination. This variation uses amaretto, almonds, and crème fraîche, but use your imagination for new flavors and textures.

1½ pounds semisweet chocolate chips
½ cup brewed espresso
½ cup amaretto liqueur
4 egg yolks
1 cup heavy or whipping cream, cold
¼ cup sugar
3 egg whites, at room temperature
Pinch of salt
1 cup lightly toasted sliced almonds
1 cup crème fraîche to garnish

Melt the chocolate chips in a heavy medium-sized saucepan over very low heat, stirring constantly. Stir in espresso and then the liqueur. Let cool to room temperature.

Add egg yolks, one at a time, beating thoroughly after each addition.

Whip the cream in a mixer bowl until thickened; gradually beat in sugar and continue beating until stiff. Beat the egg whites with the salt in another mixer bowl until stiff. Gently fold egg whites into cream.

Stir about a third of cream mixture thoroughly into the chocolate mixture; then scrape remaining cream mixture over the lightened chocolate base and fold together gently. Fold in the almonds. Pour into 8 individual dessert cups or a serving bowl. Refrigerate covered, until set, about 2 hours.

At serving time, pipe the crème fraîche decoratively over each mousse or pass the crème fraîche separately.

Serves 8

Reprinted by permission of Workman Publishing from *The Silver Palate Cookbook* by Sheila Lukins. Copyright © 1982 by Workman Publishing.

ALICE Medrich is the owner of COCOLAT, a specialty chocolate bakery in Berkeley, California. She's credited with bringing the truffles craze to this country. And she came to *Hour*'s kitchen with some delectable Valentine goodies. They were decadent, but worth every extra calorie!

Coffee Crème Anglaise

2 cups milk
4 large egg yolks
½ cup sugar
1 teaspoon vanilla plus 1 tablespoon instant espresso (stir together to dissolve)

Place a strainer over a clean bowl near stove. Scald milk in a heavy-bottomed, nonaluminum saucepan.

In a separate bowl, whisk yolks, gradually adding sugar until mixture is pale yellow and creamy. Add scalded milk gradually to yolk mixture, whisking well until all is combined.

Return mixture to saucepan and cook over medium heat, stirring constantly with a wooden spoon and reaching all over the bottom of the pan to avoid scorching. Sauce must not boil or even simmer. It will thicken slightly as it cooks.

Remove from heat when sauce coats a spoon lightly (about 165°–170°) and pour it immediately into the ready strainer and bowl. Allow to cool, then stir in vanilla and espresso. Refrigerate. Sauce should be used within 2 days to avoid spoilage.

Makes about 2 cups

ALICE MEDRICH

64   MORE RECIPES FROM HOUR MAGAZINE

Chocolate Valentine Marquise

10 ounces bittersweet or semisweet chocolate, cut into small
   pieces
4 ounces sweet butter
4 large eggs, separated
2 teaspoons powdered instand coffee dissolved in 1
   teaspoon water (optional)
⅛ teaspoon cream of tartar
2 tablespoons sugar
2 tablespoons cocoa powder

Combine chocolate and butter in a bowl set in a barely simmering pan of water. Stir frequently to hasten melting. When melted and smooth, whisk in egg yolks and coffee flavoring, if desired. Set aside.

In a clean, dry mixer bowl combine egg whites and cream of tartar. Whip until soft peaks form, then sprinkle in sugar and whip until stiff but not dry. Fold ¼ to ⅓ of the whipped egg whites into the chocolate mixture to lighten it, then fold the remaining whites into the chocolate and put immediately into a 4-cup heart-shaped (or other) mold. Chill several hours before unmolding to serve.

To serve, dip pan into hot water, wipe dry, and reverse onto a serving platter. Remove mold and dust dessert with cocoa by sifting it gently through a small fine strainer. Serve thin slices with Coffee Crème Anglaise or softly whipped cream.

If you have molded the Marquise in a bottomless mold or dessert circle, unmold and serve as follows: Dust molded Marquise with cocoa (see above) and place mold on serving platter. Warm the sides of the mold with a hot wrung-out wet towel or gently with a propane torch. Slip the mold off quickly. Refrigerate or serve.

Serves 8 to 10

ALICE MEDRICH

WHO wouldn't agree with **Ann Nickinson,** one of the owners of Manhattan's GOOD ENOUGH TO EAT restaurants, who said that food *can* comfort us and remind us of our childhood and family dining together. She and **Carrie Levin** wrote a cookbook (called *Good Enough to Eat*) filled with recipes of what they call bountiful home cooking. Here's one for a meatloaf that you'll make again and again.

Good Enough to Eat Meatloaf

2 tablespoons butter or margarine
1 large onion, chopped
1 large clove garlic, minced
1 stalk celery, sliced
1 medium green pepper, diced
2 cups sliced mushrooms (about ½ pound)
1 teaspoon pepper
One 10¾-ounce can Campbell's Condensed Tomato or
   Cream of Mushroom soup
⅓ cup ketchup
½ tablespoon mayonnaise
½ tablespoon tomato paste
1 teaspoon Worcestershire sauce
1 egg, beaten
2 tablespoons chopped fresh parsley
1 teaspoon dried basil leaves, crushed
1 teaspoon dried oregano leaves, crushed
¼ teaspoon paprika
2 tablespoons grated Parmesan cheese
½ cup fine dry breadcrumbs
2 pounds meatloaf mix (beef, pork, veal), at room
   temperature
3 slices bacon
⅓ cup water

   In a 10-inch skillet over medium heat, in hot butter, cook onion, garlic, celery, green pepper, mushrooms, and pepper until vegetables are tender, about 10 minutes. Remove from heat; cool.
   Preheat oven to 400°. In a large bowl, combine the cooled vegetables, ½ cup of the soup, and the remaining ingredients except meat, bacon, and water. Stir well.

Add meat; blend well. In 13×9-inch baking pan, shape meat mixture into 10 × 5-inch loaf. Arrange bacon slices across top.

Bake for 15 minutes. Reduce oven temperature to 350° and bake 50 minutes, or until done. Spoon off 2 tablespoons drippings; reserve. Cool meatloaf 15 minutes before slicing.

In a small saucepan over medium heat, heat remaining soup, water, and reserved drippings to boiling, stirring occasionally. Spoon over meatloaf.

Serves 8

ANN NICKINSON

Reprinted from *Good Enough to Eat*, A Fireside Book, Simon & Schuster, Inc., 1987 by Ann Nickinson and Carrie Levin.

JEAN Nidetch, whose name is synonymous with Weight Watchers, was celebrating the organization's silver anniversary on *Hour* with the book *Weight Watchers Quick and Easy Menu Cookbook*.

All the recipes in the book can each be prepared in an hour or less. After twenty-five years and over 27 million enrolled in Weight Watchers, Jean reports that weight-control meals can be tasty, nutritious, and interesting. Here's one that fits the bill and will keep you weighing in on target!

 ## Mexican Pasta Salad

For added flavor, set chili pepper on baking sheet lined with heavy-duty foil and broil 3 inches from heat source, turning frequently, until charred on all sides; let stand until cool enough to handle. Peel pepper; remove and discard stem ends and seeds. Chop pepper and proceed as directed.

> 1½ cups cooked small shell *or* elbow macaroni
> 1 medium tomato, chopped
> ¼ cup *each* diced onion and red *or* green bell pepper
> 1 medium mild *or* hot green chili pepper, seeded and chopped
> 1½ teaspoons chopped fresh cilantro (Chinese parsley)
> ½ small garlic clove, minced
> 1 tablespoon olive oil

1½ teaspoons *each* red wine vinegar and lime juice (no
   sugar added)
¼ teaspoon salt
⅛ teaspoon oregano leaves
   Dash pepper

In a large bowl (not aluminum*) combine macaroni, tomato, onion, bell pepper, chili pepper, cilantro, and garlic. In a small bowl combine remaining ingredients; pour over salad and toss to coat. Cover and refrigerate until chilled. Toss again before serving.

Serves 2
Each serving provides: 1½ bread exchanges; 2 vegetable exchanges; 1½ fat exchanges
Per serving: 204 calories; 5 g protein; 7 g fat; 30 g carbohydrate; 25 mg calcium; 279 mg sodium; 0 mg cholesterol

JEAN NIDETCH

ALEX Patout opened PATOUT'S restaurant in Louisiana in 1979. His cookbook, *Patout's Cajun Home Cooking,* is truly an authentic guide to Cajun cooking. Its purpose is to show the basics of Cajun home-style cooking as they have been passed on from generation to generation. Try his Jambalaya and redfish recipes for starters. You'll be a Cajun lover in no time at all!

♥   # Jambalaya

3 pounds fresh medium shrimp, heads on (or 2 pounds, heads off)
1 quart water
½ cup vegetable oil
3 medium yellow onions, chopped
2 large bell peppers, chopped

*It's best to marinate in glass or stainless-steel containers; acidic ingredients such as vinegar and lime juice may react with aluminum, causing color and flavor changes in foods.

5 celery ribs, chopped fine

8–10 large fresh tomatoes, peeled, seeded, and roughly chopped

2 teaspoons salt

1 teaspoon ground red pepper

½ teaspoon ground black pepper

½ teaspoon ground white pepper

1 tablespoon fresh thyme, or 2 teaspoons dried

1 tablespoon fresh basil, or 2 teaspoons dried

4–5 bay leaves

1–1½ teaspoons sugar

1 pound cooked ham, cubed

One 4-ounce can tomato sauce

1 cup chopped green onions

1 cup chopped parsley

Dehead, peel, and devein the shrimp. Place the heads and peels in a small saucepan and add the water. Bring to a slow boil over medium-high heat and let boil slowly for 15 to 20 minutes. Strain and discard the heads and peels.

Place the oil in a Dutch oven or other large heavy pot and place over medium-high heat. Add the onions, peppers, and celery and sauté, stirring often, until the vegetables are very soft, about 45 minutes. Stir in the tomatoes, salt, peppers, herbs, sugar, and shrimp stock and return to a simmer. Reduce the heat to medium and let simmer for 2 hours, stirring occasionally. This is your basic sauce; it can be prepared 1 or 2 days in advance and stored in the refrigerator.

To finish the jambalaya: Add about a pound of cubed ham and a 4-ounce can of tomato sauce to the basic sauce and simmer 45 minutes more. Meanwhile, boil or steam 2 to 3 cups raw rice.

Add the shrimp. Cook until they turn pink, 5 to 7 minutes. Stir in the green onions and parsley and let cook 1 minute more.

Place the hot cooked rice in a large bowl, pour the jambalaya base over, mix well, and serve.

Serves 6 to 8

ALEX PATOUT

Redfish with Crawfish Sauce

2 teaspoons salt

1 teaspoon ground red pepper

½ teaspoon ground black pepper
½ teaspoon ground white pepper
Dash of nutmeg
1 pint heavy cream
½ cup chopped green onions
½ cup chopped parsley
2 teaspoons dried basil or 1 tablespoon fresh
2 teaspoons dried thyme or 1 tablespoon fresh
2 pounds peeled crawfish tails, blanched
Six 8-ounce redfish fillets
Flour for dredging
1 cup margarine

Mix seasonings in a small bowl. Bring the cream to a boil in a large skillet or saucepan over medium-high heat. Add the green onions, parsley, herbs, and ½ the seasonings and continue cooking down until thick. Test the consistency by dripping from a spoon—the drops should be thick and full, and the last drop should cling to the spoon.

Add the crawfish tails and return to a simmer. The liquid from the crawfish will thin out the sauce, so continue cooking down until the mixture again becomes thick, 5 minutes at most. Keep warm in a bain-marie, if necessary, until the fish is ready.

Pat the fillets dry and sprinkle with the other half of the salt and peppers. Dredge lightly with flour. Heat the margarine in a large skillet over high heat until very hot and pan-fry the fillets until golden brown, turning just once (about 3 minutes on each side).

Place the fillets on individual plates and top with a generous amount of sauce. Be sure you distribute the crawfish evenly!

Variation

*Try substituting 2 pounds lump crabmeat for the crawfish.

Serves 6

ALEX PATOUT

Reprinted from *Patout's Cajun Home Cooking.* Copyright © 1986 by Alex Patout. Published by Random House.

PAUL Prudhomme, another Cajun master, is considered the Cajun King. His visits to *Hour*'s kitchen are always special to me and I usually try his recipes after he's been on the show. New Orleans Bread Pudding with Chantilly Cream or Lemon Sauce is a dessert that will provide a fitting end to *any* meal—Cajun or not.

New Orleans Bread Pudding

During preparation of this dish, the milk and egg mixture is too sweet and all the elements are very strong because they will be absorbed by bland bread. After baking, the result is a magnificent pudding.

          3 large eggs
     1¼ cups sugar
     1½ teaspoon vanilla extract
     1¼ teaspoon ground nutmeg
     1¼ teaspoon ground cinnamon
       ¼ cup unsalted butter, melted
          2 cups milk
       ½ cup raisins
       ½ cup coarsely chopped pecans, roasted
          5 cups very stale French or Italian bread cubes, with
            crusts on
            Lemon Sauce (recipe follows)
          1 recipe Chantilly Cream (recipe follows)

In a large bowl of an electric mixer, beat the eggs on high speed until extremely frothy and bubbles are the size of pinheads, about 3 minutes (or with a metal whisk for about 6 minutes). Add the sugar, vanilla, nutmeg, cinnamon, and butter and beat on high until well blended. Beat in the milk, then stir in the raisins and pecans.

Place the bread cubes in a greased loaf pan. Pour the egg mixture over the bread cubes and toss until the bread is soaked. Let sit until you see only a narrow bead of liquid around the pan's edges, about 45 minutes, patting the bread down into the liquid occasionally. Place in a 350° oven. Immediately lower the heat to 300° and bake until pudding is well browned and puffy, about 15 to 20 minutes more.

To serve, put 1½ tablespoons warm lemon sauce in each dessert dish, then spoon in ½ cup hot bread pudding and top with ¼ cup Chantilly Cream.

Serves 8

Chantilly Cream

⅔ cup heavy cream
1 teaspoon vanilla extract
1 teaspoon brandy
1 teaspoon Grand Marnier
¼ cup sugar
2 tablespoons dairy sour cream

Refrigerate a medium-sized bowl and beaters until very cold. Combine cream, vanilla, brandy, and Grand Marnier in the bowl and beat with electric mixer on medium speed 1 minute. Add the sugar and sour cream and beat on medium just until soft peaks form, about 3 minutes. *Do not overbeat.* [Overbeating will make the cream grainy, which is the first step leading to butter. Once grainy, you can't return it to its former consistency (but if this ever happens, enjoy it on toast!).]

Makes about 2 cups

Lemon Sauce

1 lemon, halved
½ cup water
¼ cup sugar
2 teaspoons cornstarch dissolved in ¼ cup water
1 teaspoon vanilla extract

Squeeze 2 tablespoons juice from the lemon halves and place juice in a 1-quart saucepan; add the lemon halves, water, and sugar and bring to a boil. Stir in the dissolved cornstarch and vanilla. Cook 1 minute over high heat, stirring constantly. Strain, squeezing the sauce from the lemon rinds. Serve warm.

Makes about ¾ cup

PAUL PRUDHOMME

Reprinted from *Chef Paul Prudhomme's Louisiana Kitchen.* Copyright © 1984 by Paul Prudhomme, William Morrow & Co., Inc., N.Y.

W OLFGANG Puck, who went to work in a restaurant in Southern Austria at age thirteen, has earned the reputation as America's premier chef. Besides the very successful Los Angeles restaurants SPAGO and CHINOIS, he has his own frozen food company, is author of two cookbooks and a videotape, and has two more restaurants and a brewery in the works. But his reputation and busy schedule has not changed his commitment to excellence. When he's on the show, you can't get him out of the kitchen. He doesn't even go to his dressing room, but spends all his time preparing his meal perfectly.

His incredible success is well deserved; he's a hard-working, talented man, a true perfectionist with a desire to please every customer who eats in his restaurants!

♥ ♥ Angel Hair Pasta with Shrimp, Tomato, and Basil

  3 tablespoons extra-virgin olive oil
 16 large shrimps, such as Santa Barbara
    Salt
    Freshly ground pepper
  6 cloves garlic, blanched and cut into julienne strips
  3 teaspoons chopped fresh basil, plus 4 sprigs for garnish
  4 large ripe tomatoes, peeled, seeded, and diced
  1 teaspoon minced fresh thyme leaves
  ¾ pound regular pasta, cut into angel hair noodles

Bring a large pot of water to boil with a small amount of oil.

Remove heads from shrimps and peel off shells, leaving tail shells intact. Season with salt and pepper and set aside.

Prepare sauce: Heat olive oil in a large saucepan. Sauté garlic and shrimps. Stir in basil, tomatoes, and thyme and simmer for 5 minutes.

Cook pasta al dente. Drain. Stir into tomato basil sauce until well combined.

Turn pasta onto center of 4 dinner plates. Place 4 of the shrimps around the pasta on each plate. Garnish with a sprig of basil. Serve immediately.

Serves 4

WOLFGANG PUCK

Summer Vegetables Bastille

Filling

   1 pound ground pork sausage meat
   1 egg
   1 cup breadcrumbs
   Salt
   Freshly ground pepper
   1 teaspoon chopped rosemary
   ½ teaspoon cumin
   1 teaspoon chopped fresh basil
   1 teaspoon chopped cilantro
   2 tablespoons chopped shallots

Sauce

   1 red bell pepper, chopped
   4 cloves garlic, minced
   1 teaspoon thyme leaves, chopped
   Extra-virgin olive oil
   ½ cup white wine
   ¼ cup heavy cream
   6 ounces unsalted butter, cut into pieces
   Juice and zest of 1 lime
   Salt and pepper to taste
   4 small artichokes, bottoms only
   2 medium white onions
   2 tomatoes
   1 zucchini, cut crosswise into 4 pieces
   4 small turnips
   ½ cup chicken stock
   3 tablespoons grated fresh Parmesan cheese

Make filling: Mix together sausage meat, egg, ¾ cup breadcrumbs, and salt and pepper to taste. Divide mixture into 5 equal parts. Combine 1 of the herbs with each portion. Chill until ready to use.

Prepare sauce: Sauté pepper, garlic, and thyme in a little olive oil. Deglaze pan with white wine and reduce. Add cream and bring to a boil. Remove from heat and puree in blender until smooth. Return to pan and add butter and lime juice and zest and correct seasonings. Strain and keep warm.

In boiling water, blanch artichoke bottoms for 10 minutes. Set aside. Blanch onions for about 5 minutes. Let cool and cut in half. Cut tomatoes in half. Using a teaspoon, hollow out a cavity in each of the vegetables. Spoon herbed sausage filling into each of the vegetables (which herb you pair with the vegetables is not important).

Place vegetables in a well-oiled shallow baking dish. Add chicken stock to the dish and sprinkle vegetables with remaining breadcrumbs and Parmesan cheese. Bake in a 400° oven for about 20 minutes until the sausage is cooked. Any liquid in the dish should be evaporated.

Spread 4 dinner plates with the red pepper sauce. Place 1 of each vegetable on each plate. Serve immediately.

Note: (All vegetables should be cut about 2 inches in diameter.)

Serves 4

WOLFGANG PUCK

Pecan or Walnut Tart

⅓ recipe (¾ pound) Sugar Dough
(See accompanying recipe)
2½ cups sugar
1¼ cups water
1 teaspoon fresh lemon juice
½ cup heavy cream
12 ounces walnut halves or pecans
14 tablespoons (7 ounces) unsalted butter
1 egg, lightly beaten, for egg wash
1 recipe Ganache (recipe follows) or caramel sauce

On a floured surface, roll half the sugar dough ⅜ inch thick and line a 9×1½-inch flan ring or cake pan with it. Roll the rest of the pastry into a circle 10 inches in diameter and ⅜ inch thick. Place the pastry on baking sheets and chill while preparing the filling.

Combine the sugar, water, and lemon juice in a large saucepan and stir gently to mix. Bring to a boil and cook until the mixture turns a rich caramel color, or reaches 334° on a candy thermometer. (If the caramel should crystallize as it cooks, let it continue cooking until the crystals melt again. The caramel will become quite dark and it will be necessary to add 2 to 3 tablespoons additional cream.)

Remove the pan from the heat and pour in the cream. It will bubble a lot. Swirl gently until the bubbles subside. Reserve 9 walnut halves for decoration and mix in the rest gently. Add the butter. When the butter has melted, stir the filling gently until the mixture is smooth.

Transfer the mixture to a large metal bowl and let it cool to lukewarm.

Turn the filling into the prepared flan ring. Brush the edges of the shell with egg wash and top with chilled pastry circle. Pinch the edges to seal them well, then trim away the excess dough. Cut several small slashes in the top pastry to allow the steam to escape. Chill until ready to bake.

Preheat the oven to 400°. Bake the tart in the bottom third of the oven until the crust is golden brown, about 40 to 50 minutes. Remove the tart and let cool to room temperature. Invert the tart onto a 9-inch cardboard. (If the tart sticks to the flan ring, gently heat it over low heat or use a small blow torch to loosen the caramel.) Heat the ganache in a double boiler over very low heat to a nice spreading consistency. Pour it over the top of the tart, smoothing the top and sides nicely with a large, narrow spatula.

PRESENTATION: Decorate the top of the tart with the reserved walnut halves and place it on a lovely serving plate. Serve with unsweetened lightly whipped cream if desired.

Note: The components of the tart may be made in advance and assembled when you have time.

Serves 8 to 10

WOLFGANG PUCK

Sugar Dough

1 pound unsalted butter, slightly softened
3⅓ cups (12 ounces) pastry flour
3⅓ cups (12 ounces) all-purpose flour
Pinch salt
¾ cup (6 ounces) sugar
3 egg yolks
2 tablespoons heavy cream

Cut the butter into large pieces and place the pieces in the bowl of an electric mixer fitted with a paddle or dough hooks. Add the pastry and all-purpose flour, salt and sugar. Mix on low speed until the butter is evenly distributed throughout the flour. Add the egg yolks and cream. Continue to mix on low speed until the dough pulls away from the sides of the bowl.

Remove the dough and divide it into 2 pieces. Flatten each piece into a 6-inch round. Wrap in plastic and chill for at least 2 hours or overnight. Use as needed. The dough will remain fresh for 2 or 3 days in the refrigerator; or wrap securely in plastic, then in foil, and it will keep frozen for 2 or 3 months.

Note: The dough may also be made in a food processor using the same technique, but make half a batch at a time for best results.

To prepare the dough by hand, place the flours, sugar and salt in a large bowl or on a work surface. Mix together. Cut in the butter with your fingertips. Make a well in the center of the flour mixture. Pour in the egg yolks and cream. Using your fingertips, quickly work in the flour until the dough holds together. Form the dough into rounds, wrap it in plastic wrap and chill.

Makes 2½ pounds

WOLFGANG PUCK

Ganache (Chocolate Cream)

1 pound bittersweet or semisweet chocolate
2 cups heavy cream
4 tablespoons (2 ounces) unsalted butter at room
  temperature

Cut the chocolate into small pieces and place in a metal mixing bowl. In a saucepan, bring the cream to a boil and pour it over the chocolate. Stir until the chocolate has melted. Stir in the butter until incorporated. Store the ganache in the refrigerator until you are ready to use it. It will keep for 2 to 3 weeks under refrigeration.

Reheat the ganache over hot but not boiling water until it reaches the consistency desired. (It is important that the ganache not get too hot, or the butter will separate from the base.)

Makes 1 quart

WOLFGANG PUCK

Reprinted by permission of Random House from *The Wolfgang Puck Cookbook* copyright © 1986 by Wolfgang Puck.

♥ ♥ Salmon Fillets Baked with Lemons, Scallions, and Parsley

I first tasted this dish at the home of Mike and Shelly Young, good friends and talented cooks. The presentation of the salmon was outstanding and the taste even better. When I asked about the origin of the recipe, Mike told me that he had gotten the directions while talking with an elderly fishmonger in the Pike Place Market in Seattle. The merchant swore to him that this was the easiest and best way to cook fresh salmon. I could not agree more!

Oil
2 Norwegian salmon fillets (1½ pounds each), 1 inch thick
Salt and freshly ground pepper to taste
1 cup finely chopped fresh parsley
½ cup finely chopped scallions (green onions)
3 lemons, thinly sliced
2 teaspoons very finely julienned lemon zest, for garnish
Fresh tarragon sprigs for garnish (optional)

Preheat the oven to 450°.

Line a rimless baking sheet with aluminum foil; grease it well with vegetable oil. Generously oil the salmon skin. Place the fish skin side down on the foil. Run your fingers over the flesh sides of the salmon. If you feel any bones, remove them with tweezers. Salt and pepper the fish.

Combine the parsley and scallions, and spread the mixture over the salmon. Arrange the lemon slices, slightly overlapping, over the parsley mixture.

To make the lemon zest garnish, cut several strips of lemon zest into very fine threadlike strands. Set aside.

Place the baking sheet on the center shelf of the oven and bake until the fish is opaque, about 14 minutes. Remove the sheet from the oven, remove the lemon slices, and scrape off the parsley mixture.

Cut each salmon fillet into 3 equal pieces and transfer them to a heated platter, then garnish with lemon zest and tarragon.

Serves 6

BETTY ROSBOTTOM

JEFF Smith is host of the nationally successful television show *The Frugal Gourmet* as well as a bestselling cookbook author and an ordained minister. The man who calls himself "The Frug" is always a great guest in *Hour*'s kitchen. Jeff can take a simple vegetable and prepare it in a way that will impress any guest. Each of his zucchini dishes can be used either as a first course or as a vegetable dish.

♥ ## Rolled Marinated Zucchini

4 zucchini
2 eggs, beaten
½ cup milk
2 tablespoons flour
3 tablespoons olive oil

Marinade

½ cup olive oil
2 tablespoons fresh lemon juice
Salt and pepper to taste

Slice fresh zucchini the long way, very thin (⅛ inch thick). I use an Oriental vegetable cutter for this step.

Prepare a batter of the eggs, milk, and flour. Dip the slices in the egg wash and fry in a bit of olive oil over medium-high heat. Brown lightly on both sides. Remove and place on a tray to cool.

When the slices reach room temperature, roll each up like a little jelly roll and secure with a toothpick. If the rolls appear to be too wide, they may be sliced into two rolls, each being secured with a toothpick.

Place the rolls on a serving plate. Mix the marinade and drizzle some on each.

Serves 6

JEFF SMITH

♥ ## Zucchini Fritters

3 cups coarsely grated zucchini
2 eggs, beaten
⅛ cup milk
2 teaspoons flour
  Salt and freshly ground black pepper
  Dried or fresh mint
  Olive oil for pan-frying

Grate the squash and drain in a colander for 1 hour. Mix the eggs, milk, and flour into a smooth batter. Add salt and pepper to taste. Add mint to taste. (I use about 1 teaspoon dried mint in this recipe. If using fresh mint leaf, chop about 1 tablespoon.)

Mix batter with the squash and pan-fry in small fritters in a bit of olive oil. Cook just until golden brown and serve as a first course or a vegetable dish. These can be kept warm in the oven for a bit before dinner. Be sure to cover.

Serves 6

JEFF SMITH

MARLENE Sorosky writes a syndicated column for the *Los Angeles Times* entitled "That's Entertaining." She also has a two-hour talk show on KABC radio in Los Angeles. If you can imagine improving on a near perfect food, then read on. You just mix Oreo cookies with sour cream and cream cheese to make a cream cheese cake with Oreo crust. Need I say more? I like to save this one for special guests.

Oreo Cheesecake

Crust

25 Oreo creme sandwich cookies (about 2½ cups crumbs)
4 tablespoons (½ stick) unsalted butter, melted

Make crust: Break up cookies and place in food processor fitted with metal blade; process until crumbs.
Add butter and mix until blended. Or, mix cookie crumbs and butter together in bowl.
Pour into a 9 × 3-inch or 10½ × 2-inch springform pan. Press evenly over bottom and ⅔ up sides of springform.
Refrigerate while preparing filling.

Filling

4 packages (8-ounces each) cream cheese, at room
   temperature
1¼ cups plus ¼ cup sugar
2 tablespoons all-purpose flour
4 large eggs, at room temperature
3 large egg yolks, at room temperature
⅓ cup whipping cream
2 teaspoons vanilla
1¾ cups coarsely chopped Oreo creme sandwich cookies
   (about 15 cookies)
2 cups sour cream

Make filling: Beat cream cheese in large bowl with electric mixer on medium speed until smooth. Scrape down sides. Add 1¼ cups sugar, beating mixture until light and fluffy, about 3 minutes, scraping down sides of bowl occasionally. Mix in flour. While beating continuously, add eggs and yolks; mix until smooth. Beat in whipping cream and 1 teaspoon vanilla until well blended.

Pour half the batter into prepared crust. Sprinkle with chopped Oreos. Pour remaining batter over and smooth top with spatula. Some of the Oreos may rise to the top.

Place pan on baking sheet. Bake in a 425° oven for 15 minutes. Reduce oven temperature to 225° and bake for an additional 50 minutes or until set.

Remove cake from oven and increase oven temperature to 350°. Stir together sour cream, remaining ¼ cup sugar, and 1 teaspoon vanilla in small bowl. Spread sour cream mixture evenly over cake. Return to the 350° oven; bake 7 minutes, or until sour cream begins to set. Remove from oven and cool in draft-free place to room temperature. Cover and refrigerate several hours or overnight. The cake may be refrigerated up to 3 days.

Before serving, remove sides of springform. Serve chilled.

Serves 10 to 12

MARLENE SOROSKY

Reprinted by permission of Marlene Sorosky from *The Dessert Lover's Cookbook* by Marlene Sorosky. Copyright © 1985 by Harper & Row.

S HE'S written five bestselling books and has recently released a video series called *Secrets for Entertaining*. **Martha Stewart** is a teacher extraordinaire whose name makes me think of elegant presentations. Here are two dishes that are great for entertaining.

♥
Puree of Broccoli

1 large bunch broccoli
¼ cup heavy cream
2 tablespoons butter
  Salt and freshly ground black pepper to taste
  Freshly ground nutmeg or ground cinnamon to taste

Wash broccoli. Trim off tough stems and divide stalks lengthwise. Steam broccoli until just tender; then plunge immediately into ice water to stop cooking and to preserve the bright green color. When cold, remove from water and drain.

Puree broccoli, heavy cream, butter, salt and pepper, and a pinch of nutmeg or cinnamon in a food processor until not quite smooth. Adjust seasonings to taste. Just before serving, put a little butter in a saucepan, add the puree, and gently reheat, being careful not to scorch the bottom.

Note: This can be made the day before serving and kept in the refrigerator until time to reheat.

Serves 6

MARTHA STEWART

Reprinted by permission of Martha Stewart from *Martha Stewart's Secrets for Entertaining*. Copyright © 1988 by Martha Stewart, Clarkson N. Potter, Inc., Publishers, Crown Publishers, Inc., New York.

♥ ♥   # Vegetable Mélange

20 shallots
2 pounds small white onions
4 pounds small whole red potatoes
4 pounds baby string beans, stem ends trimmed
¼ cup olive oil
4 tablespoons (½ stick) unsalted butter
1 pint sun-dried tomatoes, drained and slivered
2 tablespoons fresh thyme
Salt and freshly ground black pepper to taste

Preheat oven to 375°.
Blanch shallots and onions in boiling water for approximately 2 minutes. Drain and carefully peel, leaving the pointed ends on. Meanwhile, boil the potatoes, with skins on, until they are tender but still firm. Drain. If the potatoes are small, leave them whole; if not, halve or quarter them. Place potatoes, shallots, and onions in a roasting pan, in one layer, and drizzle with olive oil. Roast for about 15 minutes, until they are crispy outside. Remove from oven.

In another pot of boiling water, blanch the string beans for about 2 minutes, or until just tender. Plunge them into ice water to stop the cooking and to preserve the brilliant color.

Right before serving, melt the butter in a large sauté pan. Add the roasted vegetables, sun-dried tomatoes, and all other ingredients. Toss together over low heat until just heated through. Season with salt and pepper. Serve warm or at room temperature.

Serves 30

MARTHA STEWART

THAI food keeps increasing in popularity each year. And in Los Angeles, one of the favorite Thai restaurants is called TOMMY TANG'S. Master chef **Tommy Tang** has a home video, *Tommy Tang's Food Adventure,* which reveals some secrets for cooking Thai. Here's a good starter if you've never tried it. Once you have the unique ingredients (like fish sauce, black bean sauce, Thai red peppercorn, and mint leaves), the rest is easy!

♥ ♥   Chicken with Garlic Mint Sauce

    2 breasts of chicken, skinned, boned, and split
      Secret Spice Mixture (recipe follows)
   12 whole mint leaves

Sprinkle breasts with spice mixture. Grill 4 to 5 minutes per side. Slice on diagonal. Place on dish. Alternate chicken slice with mint leaf. Top with Mint Garlic Sauce (recipe follows).

Secret Spice Mixture

    1 tablespoon garlic powder
    1 tablespoon white pepper
    1 tablespoon cayenne pepper
  ½ tablespoon Thai red peppercorn

Thoroughly blend spices together.

Mint Garlic Sauce

    1 tablespoon vegetable oil
    2 tablespoons chopped garlic
    1 tablespoon chopped red serrano chile
    1 teaspoon minced red onion
    1 teaspoon fish sauce
    1 teaspoon black bean sauce
       Pinch ground black pepper
  ½ cup chicken stock
    2 tablespoons chopped mint leaves

Heat oil in a sauté pan. Sauté garlic, chile pepper, and onion for 1 minute. Add fish sauce, then black bean sauce. Sauté for 1 minute more. Add stock, mint leaves, and pepper. Simmer until thick.

Serves 2 to 4

TOMMY TANG

CHEF Tell is truly one of my favorite guests. He's an internationally renowned master of the kitchen, four-time winner of the Cordon Bleu award, and owner of the famous GRAND OLD HOUSE restaurant in the Grand Cayman Islands, British West Indies.

Every time he visits *Hour*'s kitchen he has us all laughing because he goes through his recipe faster than anyone I've ever seen and miraculously remembers every step.

On one of his week-long series he prepared the meal from appetizer through desserts. We called it his "perfect" meal, and while it may seem a bit ambitious, you'll certainly impress your guests. All the recipes are from his wonderful GRAND OLD HOUSE that Mary Ann and I recently had the pleasure of visiting.

Deep-Fried Brie

Flour for dredging
Egg wash
Breadcrumbs
Wedges of Brie or Camembert

Parsley
4 cups oil for frying

Place flour, egg, and breadcrumbs in 3 individual bowls and bread the Brie. Heat oil (in a large pot so pot is not more than half full and oil will not boil over). Heat to almost smoking point; deep-fry quickly so Brie has no time to melt or run out of breading. Dry the fried Brie on paper towel and serve immediately with parsley sprinkled on top.

Tip: You can deep-fry the parsley if you hold onto the stem and place in hot oil, but be careful—it is very dangerous and you can burn yourself easily!

CHEF TELL

Scallops in Bacon

20 slices of bacon
40 small scallops (or large ones cut in half or quarters)
Toothpicks
Oil for sautéing

Cut bacon in half crosswise; place scallops on one end and roll up. Secure with a toothpick. Sauté in a pan until bacon is crisp. Serve while hot.

Serves 4 to 6

CHEF TELL

Potato Soup

3 tablespoons butter or margarine
½ onion, chopped
1 pound leeks, sliced
6 cups chicken stock
Salt and pepper
2 pounds potatoes, sliced
2 cups cream
4 egg yolks
Marjoram

Chopped parsley
Bread croutons

Melt butter; sauté onions and leeks until tender. Add chicken stock, salt and pepper, and potatoes. Simmer until potatoes are tender. Puree.

Add binding agent made by mixing cream with egg yolks. Correct seasonings. Serve hot garnished with marjoram, chopped parsley, and bread croutons.

Serves 8

CHEF TELL

Caesar Salad

Dressing

    8 cloves garlic
    Juice of 2 limes (½ cup)
    6 anchovies
    ½ cup grated Parmesan cheese
    ¼ cup cracked black pepper
    Salt to taste
    4 egg yolks
    2 cups olive oil
    1 head romaine lettuce, washed and cut in pieces

Combine the dressing ingredients, except the oil, in a blender or food processor. Mix thoroughly. Add the oil slowly until you make the consistency of mayonnaise. Mix with the washed and cut-up pieces of romaine.

Serves 4 to 6

CHEF TELL

♥   Grand Old House Snapper (Pan-Fried)

Spice mix

    1 teaspoon paprika
    1 teaspoon sage

1 teaspoon marjoram
2 teaspoons garlic
6 scallions
1 teaspoon hot pepper
1 teaspoon black pepper
3 teaspoons lime juice
3 teaspoons olive oil
Touch of clove
One 6–8 ounce snapper or grouper
2 ounces butter for frying

Combine all herbs and spices. Mix in blender or food processor and let set for 2 to 3 hours or even overnight.

Put the spice mixture on the fish as desired, then bread as you would the Brie (see page 86). Pan-fry slowly in butter for approximately 8 minutes on each side.

Serves 1 to 2

CHEF TELL

Beef Rouladen

1 onion, chopped
Butter or oil
6 slices top round of beef
Salt and pepper
1–2 tablespoons Dijon mustard
2 tablespoons diced pickles
½ slice raw bacon, diced

Sauce

1 carrot, chopped
1 stalk celery, chopped
1 onion, chopped
1–2 slices bacon rind, diced
1 cup red wine
2 cups stock
1–2 tablespoons cornstarch, dissolved in cold water

To prepare rouladen, sauté the onion in butter until golden. Pound the meat and sprinkle with salt and pepper. Paint each side with Dijon mustard. Fill with a mixture of sautéed onion, pickles, and raw bacon. Roll and close with a toothpick.

Sauté the beef on all sides in hot fat until browned. Add the chopped vegetables and the bacon rind for the sauce. Stir and brown a little. Add red wine and stock; braise until the meat is tender. Remove the meat and strain the sauce. Thicken with the cornstarch mixture.

Serve the meat with the sauce and mashed potatoes.

Variations

Fill with ground meat or bread stuffing.

Serves 6

CHEF TELL

Chocolate Parfait with Vanilla Sauce

    2 pounds bittersweet chocolate
    6 ounces sweet butter
   12 egg yolks
    1 shot peppermint
    1 shot dark rum
    1 shot Grand Marnier
    1 shot Cointreau
    1 shot cognac
      Grated rind of 2 lemons
    1 cup peeled and shirred pistachios
    2 cups heavy cream, beaten (whipped)
      Vanilla Sauce (made by melting 2 cups vanilla ice cream)

Melt the chocolate in a large bowl over boiling water, then add butter, egg yolks, all the liquor, grated rind, and pistachios. When all folded under, add the whipped cream, put in loaf pan, and chill overnight. When removing, let hot water run over the bottom of loaf pan (upside down), then let fall out. Place on large serving tray and garnish with Vanilla Sauce.

Serves 8 to 10

CHEF TELL

Ma Maison Chicken Salad

*Ma Maison's chicken salad, like Nathan's hot dogs or Chasen's chili, is an
institution. On the menu since the restaurant opened in 1973, this tangy version
of an American classic has remained the most popular dish at lunch.*

*With a loaf of French bread, a light white wine, and a fruit dessert, it would
be a perfect hot weather lunch or supper. Store leftovers in the refrigerator for great
chicken salad sandwiches.*

> One 3–3½-pound chicken
> 10 cups chicken stock or canned chicken broth
> 1 red or golden Delicious apple, peeled, cored, and diced
> 2 celery stalks, peeled and cubed
> 1 tablespoon capers, drained
> ½ cup mayonnaise
> 2 tablespoons grainy mustard
> 2 tablespoons Dijon mustard
> Salt and freshly ground pepper to taste
> Fresh lemon juice to taste
> 1 head butter or limestone lettuce, washed and dried
> ¼ cup vinaigrette
> 2 hard-boiled eggs, halved (garnish)
> 2 tomatoes, cut in wedges (garnish)
> 2 bell peppers, sliced (garnish)
> 8 ounces green beans, blanched (garnish)

Combine the chicken and stock in a large pot. Bring to a simmer and cook
uncovered for 20 minutes over low heat.

Remove the chicken from the pot to cool. When it's cool enough to handle
but still warm, remove and discard the skin. Pull the meat from the bones and
shred by hand into bite-sized pieces. Place the pieces in a large mixing bowl.

Add the apple, celery, capers, mayonnaise, and mustards to the chicken and combine gently. Taste and adjust seasonings with salt, pepper, and lemon juice.

Break the lettuce into bite-sized pieces and place in another mixing bowl. Toss with the vinaigrette.

To serve: Divide the lettuce among 4 serving plates. Top each with a serving of chicken salad and garnish as desired. Serve at room temperature.

Serves 4

PATRICK TERRAIL AND JEAN-PIERRE LEMANISSIER

M**ARY Lou Warren** was the reigning bake-off winner for Pillsbury when she visited *Hour*'s kitchen. She made her winning recipe, Apple Nut Lattice Tart, and with just one bite, I knew why she had won!

Apple Nut Lattice Tart

One 15-ounce package Pillsbury All Ready Pie Crust

Filling

3–3½ cups thinly sliced, peeled apples
½ cup sugar
3 tablespoons golden raisins
3 tablespoons chopped walnuts or pecans
½ teaspoon cinnamon
¼–½ teaspoon grated lemon peel
2 teaspoons lemon juice
1 egg yolk, beaten
1 teaspoon water

Glaze

¼ cup powdered sugar
1–2 teaspoons lemon juice

Prepare pie crust according to package directions for a 2-crust pie using a 10-inch tart pan with a removable bottom or a 9-inch pie pan. Heat oven to 400°. Place 1 prepared crust in pan; press in the bottom and sides of pan. Trim edges if necessary.

In a large bowl, combine apples, sugar, raisins, walnuts, cinnamon, lemon peel, and 2 teaspoons lemon juice. Spoon into pie crust–lined pan.

To make a lattice top, cut remaining crust into ½-inch-wide strips. Arrange strips in lattice design over apple mixture. Trim and seal edges. In a small bowl, combine egg yolk and water; gently brush over lattice. Bake at 400° for 40 to 60 minutes, or until golden brown and apples are tender. Cool 1 hour.

In a small bowl, combine glaze ingredients; drizzle over slightly warm tart. Cool; remove sides of pan.

Tip: Cover pie with foil during last 15 to 20 minutes of baking if necessary to prevent excessive browning.

Serves 8

MARY LOU WARREN

BARBARA Zara wrote the bestselling book *I Left My Fat Behind* and now runs a successful weight-loss program based in Fort Lauderdale, Florida. Her recipe for Best Ever Lemon Chicken is healthy for your heart, tasty, and low in calories. What more could you ask for?

 ## Best Ever Lemon Chicken

4 skinless chicken breasts (about 1½ pounds)
Salt, pepper, and paprika for seasoning
¾ cup water, divided
¼ cup white wine
1 teaspoon chicken bouillon powder
¼ cup lemon juice

2 teaspoons flour
1 lemon, thinly sliced

Preheat oven to 375°. Spray a frying pan with PAM. Season chicken breasts to taste with salt, pepper, and paprika. Heat frying pan and sauté chicken until nicely browned (about 10 minutes), adding about ¼ cup water near the end of the cooking time to loosen meat from the pan.

Remove chicken breasts to a shallow baking dish. To the pan juices, add the white wine, ½ cup water, and chicken bouillon, and heat through. Meanwhile, mix the lemon juice and flour in a cup. Pour into the frying pan and stir until sauce is thickened.

Pour sauce over chicken, top with lemon slices, and bake for 20 minutes.

Serves 4
One Serving: 4 oz. protein, 1 slice thin diet bread (179 calories per serving)

BARBARA ZARA

2

CELEBRITIES

As I said in the first *Hour Magazine* cookbook, celebrity cooking spots are usually more fun than the sit-down interviews because a vulnerable side of their personality is usually revealed when behind a steaming pot or a sizzling frying pan! Here are many of the people you love to watch each week on your TV set—and surprisingly enough, many of them are excellent cooks.

♥ ♥ ## Vegetables Lo Mein

Fresh Chinese noodles (Naki Yaki Udon, no egg noodles)
Extra oil to stir-fry vegetables
1 leaf of cabbage, thinly sliced
3 carrots, julienne cut
2 stalks celery, sliced diagonally
1 bunch green onions, diagonally cut *(you may also use your
favorite vegetables)*

Sauce

4 tablespoons soy sauce
1 tablespoon sugar
4 tablespoons oyster sauce
4 tablespoons peanut oil

Cook noodles in a large pot of boiling water until translucent and firm.
Drain. Meanwhile, in wok, heat 1 tablespoon oil and stir-fry cabbage 1 minute.
Remove from wok and set aside.
Add more oil if necessary and stir-fry carrots, celery, and green onions.
Make sauce: Combine soy sauce, sugar, oyster sauce, and peanut oil. Add sauce
and noodles and toss gently. Add cabbage and toss again.
Serve immediately.

Serves 4

LYLE ALZADO

TERI Austin, whom you know from *Knots Landing,* was raised in Toronto, and actually was a talk-show host herself in the early eighties on a Canadian show called *The Thrill of a Lifetime.* It's always fun to have Terri on because she's been in my shoes. She has a comic side to her personality that rarely gets revealed on *Knots Landing;* however, I was able to see a part of it when she made her poached salmon entrée.

♥   Angel Hair Pasta with Tomatoes and Feta

  1 pound capellini or angel hair pasta
¼ cup olive oil
  8 ounces feta cheese, cubed
  2 cups Italian plum tomatoes, chopped
½ cup sliced black olives
¼ cup sliced red onions
¼ cup chopped fresh basil
  1 tablespoon minced garlic
    Salt and pepper to taste

Cook pasta. Toss with oil, then all of the remaining ingredients. Serve immediately.

Serves 8

TERI AUSTIN

♥ ♥   Poached Salmon with Basil

  2 salmon steaks
    Olive oil
  2 large basil leaves
    Sliced lemon
    Salt and pepper to taste
  1 cup white wine

1 cup water
Parsley (garnish)

Place salmon steaks in a baking dish. Brush with olive oil. Top each steak with a basil leaf and a slice of lemon. Season with salt and pepper. Pour wine and water in the dish and broil for 8 to 10 minutes. Garnish with parsley.

Serves 2

TERI AUSTIN

DOUG Barr, who you know from *The Fall Guy* and *The Wizard,* is not just another handsome actor. He's also a whiz in the kitchen who's conscious of healthy eating habits, as you can see by his recipe for roasted lemon chicken.

♥ ## Roasted Chicken in Lemon Sauce

One 4–5-pound roasting chicken
12 lemons, juiced
Salt and pepper
Olive oil
2 tablespoons chopped parsley
2 tablespoons chopped basil
2 tablespoons chopped dill
2 tablespoons cilantro
1 cup Greek Kalamata olives
½ lemon
½ cup sun-dried tomatoes
Lemon Basting Sauce (recipe follows)

Place chicken in a large bowl. Pour lemon juice over chicken. Let marinate overnight.
Next day, remove chicken from juice.
Preheat oven to 350°. Salt and pepper entire bird. Rub with olive oil. Sprinkle with small amount of herbs. Toss olives with oil and remaining herbs. Then stuff into cavity.
Place ½ lemon into cavity opening. Stuff sun-dried tomatoes under the skin of the breast.
Roast chicken at 350° for 2 hours, basting with Lemon Basting Sauce.

Lemon Basting Sauce

      2 tablespoons butter
      Reserved ½ lemon from roasted chicken
      1 tablespoon minced garlic
      3 tablespoons honey
      1 tablespoon Dijon mustard
      1 tablespoon lemon marmalade
      Salt and pepper

Melt butter in medium saucepan.
Add remaining ingredients. Heat until thoroughly blended, stirring often.

Serves 6

DOUG BARR

BRIAN Boitano brought America its first Gold Medal of the 1988 Winter Olympic Games. He proudly said it was the best he's ever skated in his life. After sixteen years of skating (he began at eight when he asked his father to take him ice skating) and rigorous training, he was able to realize his achievement in one brilliant 4½-minute performance.

Brian told me that he has another passion too, and that's Italian food. He hopes someday to open up an Italian restaurant in San Francisco; in the meantime, he gave us some of his basic recipes with one suggestion: Lots of oil is Italian!

Pasta Carbonara

      1 pound bacon, diced
      2 tablespoons butter
      2 eggs
      1 pound pasta (Brian uses spaghetti)
      1 pound freshly grated Parmesan cheese

Simmer diced bacon in a skillet until cooked but not crisp; add butter.
Take off heat and cool to room temperature.
Beat the eggs. Add bacon mixture to eggs and stir.

Cook pasta in plenty of boiling salted water until al dente.

When pasta is cooked, alternately stir in bacon mixture and Parmesan. Stir in quickly and serve immediately.

Serves 8 to 10

BRIAN BOITANO

Vegetable Boitano

Generous amount of oil
½ Spanish onion, sliced
1 clove garlic, diced
1 red pepper, sliced
1 green pepper, sliced
1 handful fresh parsley
2 zucchini, sliced
5 small tomatoes, sliced
Butter
Salt
Lots of pepper
Juice of ½ lemon

Heat oil in a skillet. Add onion and garlic, stirring constantly over medium-high heat. Add sliced peppers and fresh parsley. Cook until soft. Add sliced zucchini, then tomatoes. Simmer until ready to eat. Then add butter, salt and pepper to taste, and lemon juice. Serve.

Serves 4 to 6

BRIAN BOITANO

♥ ♥   Beverly Sanders's Surprise Chicken

1 whole roasting chicken (3–4 pounds)
1 tablespoon garlic powder
1 tablespoon ginger powder
1 medium onion, sliced
2 zucchini, cut in strips
2 carrots, cut in strips
1 cup diet orange soda (your favorite brand)
4 tablespoons soy sauce

Rub chicken with garlic and ginger powders. Place on rack in a roasting pan. Arrange vegetables around the base. Pour orange soda and soy sauce over the chicken. Bake at 350° for 1½ to 2 hours, basting every 20 minutes with pan drippings.

Serves 4

JOEL BROOKS

Antipasto Salad

1 head romaine lettuce
1 head red leaf lettuce

½ cup Italian salad dressing
3 tomatoes, cut in wedges
1 cup marinated artichoke hearts
2 hard boiled eggs, quartered
¼ pound salami
¼ pound mortadella
¼ pound sliced provolone cheese
Chopped parsley
1 cup Italian olives
¼ pound Italian ham
¼ pound sliced mozzarella cheese
Oregano flakes

Shred lettuces. Toss with dressing. Place on the bottom of a large platter. Arrange remaining items on and around the lettuce.

Serves 6 to 8

LEO BUSCAGLIA

♥ Risotto alla Milanese

¼ cup sliced porcini or domestic variety mushrooms
¼ cup chopped onion
¼ cup Italian sausage (preferably small thin type), cut in pieces
3 tablespoons olive oil
2 cloves garlic, chopped
1 cup risotto (Italian long-grain rice)
3–4 cups hot beef broth
Large pinch saffron threads in ⅛ cup water
¼ cup grated Parmesan cheese

In a large pot sauté mushrooms, onion, and sausage in olive oil for 2 to 3 minutes. Add garlic and continue sautéing for 2 to 3 minutes more. Stir in rice. When rice is well coated, slowly add the broth, a ladleful at a time, allowing the rice to absorb the excess liquid before adding the next. The mixture must be stirred *constantly*.

When the rice is almost al dente, add the saffron and water and stir well. A little more liquid may be added according to how moist you want the rice. Add cheese, stir again, and serve immediately.

While this recipe is a bit time-consuming (20 to 25 minutes), it's well worth it!

Serves 4

LEO BUSCAGLIA

DEAN Butler was best known as Almanzo Wilder on *Little House on the Prairie,* and now he's playing Jeff "Moondoggie" Griffin each week in *The New Gidget.* He was born in Canada and spent his childhood in San Francisco, where the weather is often a bit nippy. Dean says that soup soothes him and feels nurturing to him. He included a recipe for ice cream, because, he says, that can be comforting too!

Beef Soup

5 pounds lean beef stew meat
4 tablespoons oil
6 medium onions, chopped
4 cans Campbell's Consommé
4 cups water
Four 28-ounce cans whole packed tomatoes
4 cups grated carrots
1 head cabbage

Cut stew meat into bite-sized pieces. Put oil in bottom of soup pot and sear meat 5 to 6 minutes. Add onions and cook for an additional 5 minutes. Add consommé and water. Then add tomatoes and cook for ½ hour. Grate carrots and chop cabbage. Add to soup and cook for 1 hour.

Serves 12 to 16

DEAN BUTLER

Homemade Banana Ice Cream

         12 ripe bananas
          2 quarts whipping cream
      1½ cups sugar
          2 tablespoons lemon juice
         ½ teaspoon salt
          2 tablespoons vanilla
  25 to 30 pounds chopped ice
          5 pounds rock salt

Blend all bananas in food processor until thick mixture. Put banana mixture in bottom of ice cream maker. Add whipping cream, sugar, lemon juice, salt, and vanilla. There should be about 2 inches of space between the top of the mixture and the top of the freezer.

Fill ice cream maker with an ice and rock salt mixture of 2 ice to 1 rock salt ratio. Crank freezer handle about 15 to 20 minutes, refilling around ice cream container with ice and rock salt mixture.

Makes 1 gallon

DEAN BUTLER

THE multitalented **Charo** is always a great guest in the *Hour Magazine* kitchen. When she visited us she had just opened a restaurant in Hawaii, on the island of Kauai. So she brought us some of her tried and true recipes—Fish Charo and Stuffed Mushrooms à la Charo.

♥ ♥ ## Fish Charo with Hollandaise Sauce

   One 8-ounce fillet (mahi mahi, ono, or wahoo)
      1 ounce crabmeat or 1 crab leg
      2 asparagus spears
         Hollandaise Sauce (recipe follows)

Broil fish until cooked completely (3 minutes per side). Top with crab, asparagus, and Hollandaise Sauce.

Serves 1

Hollandaise Sauce

    3 egg yolks
    ½ teaspoon salt
      Pinch cayenne pepper
    1 tablespoon lemon juice
    8 tablespoons butter cut into small pieces

Put egg yolks, salt, pepper, and lemon juice in a small pan over low heat. Beat with a wire whisk until eggs and seasonings are well blended and the egg yolks have thickened to the consistency of heavy cream. Add the butter piece by piece until it has been absorbed by the eggs. The sauce should be of a consistency that coats the whisk heavily.

Makes 1 cup

CHARO

Stuffed Mushrooms à la Charo

    ¼ cup chopped onion
    ¼ cup chopped celery
    ⅛ cup butter
    ½ teaspoon salt
    ½ teaspoon pepper
      Dash cayenne pepper
    ½ pound medium shrimp, chopped, peeled, and deveined
    5 slices white bread, crusts removed
    ¼ cup mayonnaise
    1 beaten egg
   16 medium-sized or large mushrooms
      Butter
      Grated cheddar cheese
    2 gloves garlic, minced

Sauté onion and celery in ⅛ cup butter. Add ½ teaspoon salt and pepper. Sprinkle cayenne pepper over mixture. Sauté onion-celery mix for 5 minutes. Chop the shrimp and mix with onion-celery mixture. Sauté for 5 minutes, or until shrimp is pink. Let cool.

In another bowl, dice 5 slices white bread and mix onion-celery mixture into bread. To bread-onion mix, add ¼ cup mayonnaise and 1 beaten egg. Clean mushrooms and remove stems. Sauté in butter and garlic for about 3 minutes. Absorb excess butter. Over each mushroom, put a little of the bread mixture and then sprinkle a little cheddar cheese on top of that. Bake mushrooms for 10 minutes in a 400° oven.

Serves 4

CHARO

M ERRY Clayton was born on Christmas Day and played Detective Verna Dee Johnson on *Cagney and Lacey*. But you may know her from her talents as a singer: She sang on the track of one of the hottest movies of the year, *Dirty Dancing*. Her irish stew was made in honor of St. Patrick's Day.

♥ ♥   **Gaelic Beef**
(Bergin's True Irish Stew)

2 pounds boned stewing steak
2 tablespoons cooking oil
3 bay leaves
1 large onion, sliced
2 tablespoons flour
½ cup Guinness
¼ cup port
½ cup water
   Salt and pepper
1 tablespoon chopped parsley
½ pound carrots
1 cup soaked pitted prunes
1 cup small stewing onions

Trim the meat and cut into convenient serving pieces. Do not make them too small. Heat the oil and put in the bay leaves. Let them crackle, then put the lid on. Add the beef and fry on both sides; when half done, add the sliced onion and let the onion gently color to a pale gold. Sprinkle the flour over the beef and onion mixture, and let it brown, then add the Guinness, the port, and water. A little more liquid may be needed, in which case make it water or stock to just cover the meat. Season to taste with salt and pepper and add the parsley and carrots cut into circles. Put the lid on and braise in a slow to moderate oven (275°–300°) for about 2 hours. Stir it around at least once and add a little more liquid if it is drying up.

Allow the stew to cool or store it cold. When gently reheating the stew, add the cup of soaked and stoned prunes plus the cup of small stewing onions after they have both been warmed.

Serves 4

MERRY CLAYTON

I F you dropped by Kelly's Diner to visit Ruby Anderson on *General Hospital,* what do you think she'd make? Well, believe it or not, **Norma Connolly** *does* cook at home and she brought one of her favorite chicken recipes to the *Hour Magazine* kitchen for me and all her dedicated soap opera fans!

Chicken Paprika

½ onion, minced
2 tablespoons sweet butter
Whole 3½-pound chicken, cut in parts
½ cup chicken broth
3–6 tablespoons real Hungarian paprika
½ cup sour cream
1 pint sweet cream

Brown minced onion in butter very slowly. Add chicken parts and brown equally slowly. Add chicken broth. Sprinkle with paprika, cover, and cook for 20 minutes.

Remove chicken from pan. Beat sour cream and sweet cream together in pan. Put chicken back in for a few minutes more and sprinkle with "tons" of paprika.

Serve with spaetzle and cucumber salad (slice cucumbers thin, add 1 tablespoon sugar and 3 tablespoons white wine vinegar).

Serves 4 to 6

NORMA CONNOLLY

WHEN **Bob Conrad** was my co-host, his daughter **Nancy** visited *Hour*'s kitchen and made Cream of Mushroom Soup. Bob always likes to get his family involved with all his projects and daughter Nancy was no exception. On the set of Bob's *High Mountain Rangers,* he just happened to hire the best caterer he knew. And that, of course, was Nancy. After tasting her savory soup, I can understand why Bob made that choice!

Cream of Mushroom Soup

1 medium onion
¼ cup butter
½ pound fresh mushrooms
1 cup butter
½ cup flour
1 quart half-and-half
1 quart rich chicken stock
  Salt and pepper to taste

Finely chop onion and sauté in ¼ cup butter until soft.

Clean and finely chop mushrooms. Sauté in same pan as the onions (adding more butter if necessary), stirring constantly, until the liquid begins to come out of the mushrooms. Stop at this point and set aside in a bowl.

Prepare a rich cream sauce: Melt 1 cup butter; stir in flour. Cook this for 2 to 3 minutes over low heat, stirring constantly. Add half-and-half and stir until it begins to thicken. Then add chicken stock; continue cooking and stirring until it boils. The resulting sauce should not be too thick . . . as in SOUP. You can control the thickness by adding or subtracting broth.

Add mushroom and onion mixture to the soup. Add salt and pepper to taste. Can be frozen in jars.

Serves 8 to 10

NANCY CONRAD

Crawfish Étouffée

1 cup unsalted butter
1 cup white onions, chopped finely
½ cup celery, chopped finely
1 cup shallots, chopped finely
1 teaspoon minced garlic
2 tablespoons sifted flour
1 cup whole peeled tomatoes, drained and chopped
2 cups fish stock
1 teaspoon salt
1 teaspoon black pepper
  Dash cayenne pepper
1 tablespoon Worcestershire sauce
2 cups crawfish tails, cleaned

Melt butter in a cast-iron Dutch oven. Add onions, celery, shallots, and garlic. Sauté 10 minutes. Gradually add the flour. Cook over medium heat for approximately 30 minutes, until the mixture has turned medium brown. Stir constantly. Add the tomatoes. Cook for 10 minutes. Gradually stir in the fish stock. Add the salt, peppers, and the Worcestershire sauce. Simmer for 10 minutes. Add the crawfish and cook 15 minutes more. Serve over hot rice.

Serves 4

RITA COOLIDGE

♥ ♥ ## Peanut Sauce

        2 onions, peeled and cut into quarters
        5 cloves garlic
        3 tablespoons ginger
        2 tablespoons oil
       12 ounces unsalted peanuts
        3 teaspoons curry powder
      2–3 teaspoons chili powder
        1 cup mango chutney
        3 cups water
        1 cup white vinegar

Chop onions, garlic, and ginger in food processor; sauté in oil until brown.
Chop peanuts and add to pan with curry and chili powder and sauté for 2 to 3 minutes.
Add chutney, water, and vinegar; lower heat and simmer for 20 minutes.
Serve as condiment or with barbecued chicken, beef, and lamb.

Makes 3 to 4 cups

JOHN DAVIDSON

native of Brooklyn, New York, of Italian descent who made his mother and sister laugh when he was still very young is today one of America's funniest men. Earlier this year **Dom DeLuise** wrote his own cookbook, *Eat This . . . It'll Make You Feel Better.* He says that cooking, especially chopping ingredients, is very therapeutic for him. Specialties of the DeLuise house are Italian and Chinese cuisine.

Dom, who's always a pleasure to be around, offered two of his easier recipes, Seafood on Toast and Caponata.

♥ ♥

Dom's Seafood on Toast

        4 tablespoons olive oil
        1 onion, cut in crescents
        4 garlic cloves, minced
        1 red bell pepper, chopped
    One 28-ounce can crushed tomatoes
        1 large fresh tomato, chopped
        ½ cup white wine
          Salt and pepper
       2½ pounds assorted seafood (halibut, sole, red mullet,
             scallops, shrimp, and squid)
        6 slices hot toasted bread

Heat 2 tablespoons olive oil in a large pot. Add onion, garlic, and red pepper; gently sauté for 5 minutes. Add canned and fresh tomatoes, wine, salt, and pepper; slowly bring to a boil.

In remaining oil, gently sauté seafood, then add to tomato mixture. Cover and simmer for 30 minutes, or until seafood is tender.

Place slice of hot toast in bottom of each soup bowl; pour seafood stew over it. Serve immediately.

Serves 6

DOM DELUISE

♥

Dom's Caponata
(Eggplant with Tomatoes)

        6 tablespoons olive oil, divided
        1 eggplant, diced

2 onions, finely chopped
2 stalks celery, chopped
1 cup pitted black olives
5 tomatoes, skinned and chopped
  Salt and pepper
2 tablespoons sugar
6 tablespoons wine vinegar
3 tablespoons capers

Heat 3 tablespoons olive oil in a skillet and fry eggplant until golden brown. Drain on paper towels. Heat remaining oil in a heavy pan, add onion; gently sauté for 15 minutes. Add celery, olives, tomatoes, pinch of salt and pepper, sugar, vinegar, capers, and eggplant. Cook for 10 minutes until vinegar has evaporated. Remove from heat and let cool. Chill; serve cold.

Serves 6 to 8

DOM DELUISE

S HE was a Broadway veteran spending years in such hits as *The Sound of Music.* She also took some time out to work with the New York City Opera Company, and she was the first co-host with David Hartman on *Good Morning America.* But you loved her and laughed with her on *The Ted Knight Show* as Ted's TV wife.

Below are her recipes for two basics—chopped salad and baked potatoes—and you don't have to be as multitalented as **Nancy Dussault** to pull them off!

Italian Chopped Salad

As this is a filling and compact salad, the portions should be small. It also serves very nicely as a summer luncheon with good, crusty bread, a cool bottle of wine, fruit, and cheese. Have the cheese and salami sliced thinly at your market. The thin slices a commercial slicer can produce are difficult to achieve at home.

  4 cups chopped iceberg lettuce
  1 scallion
  2 tomatoes
  ¼ teaspoon salt

3 ounces Italian salami, thinly sliced
3 ounces provolone cheese, thinly sliced
   About 5 ounces garbanzo beans (chick peas)
¼ scant cup Parmesan cheese
½ cup basic vinaigrette
   Salt and pepper
18 Italian or Greek black olives

Chop lettuce finely and place in plastic bag. Finely chop scallion, including green stalk; add to the lettuce. Seal and refrigerate.

Cut tomatoes into small cubes and salt.

Bring salami and cheese to room temperature; separate. Cut into very thin strips about 2 inches long. Cover with plastic and refrigerate.

Drain garbanzo beans well; cover. Set aside. Salad may be prepared in advance to this point. Cover and refrigerate ingredients.

In large salad bowl, combine lettuce, salami, cheese, garbanzo beans, Parmesan cheese, and vinaigrette, reserving 1 teaspoon vinaigrette for tomatoes. Mix well.

Correct seasoning. Divide among 6 salad plates.

Drain tomatoes, mix with a teaspoon of dressing, and place small amount on top of each salad along with 3 olives on top of each serving.

Serves 4 to 6

NANCY DUSSAULT

Baked Potatoes with Sour Cream and Red Salmon Caviar

2 medium Idaho baking potatoes
   Salt and freshly ground pepper
⅔ cup sour cream
3 ounces red salmon caviar
1 tablespoon fresh snipped chives

Preheat the oven to 400°. Scrub the potatoes and dry them. Pierce each potato with the sharp point of a knife. Place the potatoes on an oven rack and cook for 40 minutes, or until tender. Cut crosses in the top of the potatoes and press potatoes open. Season with salt and pepper and spoon equal amounts of the sour cream and caviar over the potatoes and sprinkle with the chives.

Serves 2

NANCY DUSSAULT

♥ ♥

Poulet Orientale

1 tablespoon minced ginger
1 tablespoon minced garlic
¼ cup olive or peanut oil
One 2-pound boneless breast of chicken, skinned and diced
8 cherry tomatoes, peeled
1 cup broccoli florets
4 scallions, cut in 1" strips
1 cup asparagus, peeled and cut in 1" strips
1 cup summer squash (yellow), julienned
1 cup button mushrooms, stemmed
½ cup yellow bell pepper, julienned
½ cup red bell pepper, julienned
⅓ cup soy sauce
1 tablespoon olive or peanut oil
1 cup snow peas, trimmed

Sauté ginger and garlic in oil. Add chicken. Stir-fry for 5 to 6 minutes. Remove chicken. Add vegetables (except snow peas); stir-fry quickly 2 to 3 minutes. Add chicken and soy sauce. Reduce heat to simmer. Cover and cook for an additional three to four minutes. In a separate sauté pan, heat I tablespoon oil. Sauté peas for 1 minute. Stir into chicken mixture and serve immediately with rice.

Serves 6 to 8

JOAN FONTAINE

♥ ## Linguine and Shrimp alla Puttanesca

2 cloves garlic, minced
¼ teaspoon hot pepper flakes
2 tablespoons oil
1 pound jumbo shrimp, cleaned and deveined
2 cups marinara sauce
2 tablespoons capers
⅓ cup chopped black olives
Salt and pepper to taste
1 pound linguine, cooked
Grated Romano cheese

Sauté garlic and pepper flakes in oil for 1 minute. Add shrimp. Brown on each side (approximately 2 to 3 minutes).

Add marinara sauce, capers, and olives. Simmer 8 to 10 minutes. Add seasonings. Serve over hot linguine. Top with grated cheese.

Serves 8

SAMANTHA FOX

DANNY Frischman, who plays the nerd Arvid Engen on *Head of the Class,* got his start as a stand-up comic appearing in college coffeehouses. Originally from New Jersey, he brought a traditional recipe for noodle pudding from his grandmother.

 ## Grandmother Frischman's Noodle Pudding

One 12-ounce box wide noodles
One 13-ounce can yellow cling sliced peaches in heavy syrup
2 eggs, beaten
1 tablespoon safflower oil
1 small can crushed pineapple
1 cup raisins
4 tablespoons brown sugar
1 teaspoon cinnamon
½ cup chopped walnuts
Rind from 1 California lemon
½ cup orange juice

Cook and drain noodles.
Oil casserole dish.
Cut peaches in bite-sized pieces and mix with all ingredients except noodles. Add noodles last to bowl with above ingredients. Mix thoroughly. Pour into oiled casserole.
Bake at 350° for 1 to 1¼ hours.

Serves 8 to 10

DANNY FRISCHMAN

STEPHEN Furst, whose only acting experience before the movie *Animal House* included performing in civic and college plays and dinner club musical comedies, played the very funny Dr. Elliot Axelrod in TV's *St. Elsewhere*. But he delivered pizzas when he first came to Los Angeles, then became manager of an Italian restaurant and learned about cooking. And he told me that he does all the cooking in his house for his wife and two sons.

In the *Hour Magazine* kitchen, Dr. Axelrod prescribed Pumpkin Soup instead of the more traditional chicken soup. Try it!

Pumpkin Soup

¼ pound (1 stick) sweet butter
One 1-pound can pumpkin
8 ounces chicken stock
1 pint half-and-half
4 tablespoons chives, chopped
Salt and pepper

Melt butter in medium saucepan. Add pumpkin, chicken stock, half-and-half, and 3 tablespoons chives. Heat thoroughly on low heat. Season with salt and pepper. Garnish with remaining chives.

Serves 2 to 4

STEPHEN FURST

BEVERLY Garland was in the original movie *Invasion of the Body Snatchers* and one of the stars of TV's *Scarecrow and Mrs. King*. She's a hotel owner—The Beverly Garland Howard Johnson's in North Hollywood and The Beverly Garland Motor Lodge in Sacramento—and owns as well a restaurant called Fillmore's in Sacramento. The last time she visited *Hour*'s kitchen she brought her husband Fillmore Crank and made a bean dip named after her daughter, Carrington!

Carrington's Bean Dip

Two 10½-ounce cans Frito's Bean Dip
1 cup sour cream

One 8-ounce package Philadelphia Cream Cheese
One 1¼-ounce package taco seasoning mix (Lawry's or
    Schilling)
20 drops Tabasco sauce
½ cup green onions, finely cut (approximately 1 bunch)
1 small can olives, chopped
½ pound sharp cheddar cheese, grated
½ pound Monterey Jack cheese, grated

Mix everything **except last 2 cheeses** with electric mixer. Pour into ungreased shallow 2-quart casserole and top with cheeses.

Bake at 350° for 15 minutes, or until cheese is melted. Serve with tortilla chips.

Serves 12 (less if you give everyone time)

BEVERLY GARLAND

MARLA Gibbs is the star of the hit sitcom *227*. Yet she always likes to refer to herself as a part of an ensemble effort. For years, you loved her as Florence, the sassy housekeeper in *The Jeffersons,* and Marla says that both characters (Mary in *227* and Florence in *The Jeffersons*) are down-to-earth, even though they both had a quick and sharp tongue.

When she's not busy working at the studio, she's busy running her supper club, MARLA'S MEMORY LANES, in Los Angeles.

♥ ♥   **Stir-Fried Shrimp and Vegetables**

1 tablespoon margarine
1 tablespoon olive oil
1 cup cauliflower florets
1 cup sliced carrots
1 small red onion, chopped
1 tablespoon chopped ginger
1 red bell pepper, chopped
1 green bell pepper, chopped
1 cup broccoli florets
1 tablespoon chopped garlic
1 cup snow peas

1½ cups bean sprouts
1 dash Vegit (vegetable seasoning)
1 tablespoon tamari soy sauce (low salt soy sauce)
1 dozen jumbo shrimp, peeled and deveined
1 cup sliced mushrooms
1 tablespoon sweet cooking rice wine

Put margarine and oil into wok. Heat and add cauliflower and carrots. Stir-fry for 5 minutes.

Add red onion, ginger, and red and green bell peppers. Stir-fry for 1 minute.

Add broccoli and garlic. Stir-fry for 2 more minutes; then add snow peas and bean sprouts and stir-fry for 2 minutes more.

Add Vegit and tamari soy sauce; add shrimp, mushrooms, and rice wine. Cook until shrimp are pink or stir-fry for 5 minutes more.

Serve with brown rice.

Serves 6 to 8

MARLA GIBBS

Marla's Lemon Peach Pie

One 14-ounce can sweetened condensed milk
Juice of 1 lemon
One 16-ounce can sliced peaches in heavy syrup, drained and chopped
One 8-ounce package nondairy whipped topping
Ready made graham cracker pie crust

Put the sweet condensed milk into a large bowl and add lemon juice, peaches, and whipped topping.

Blend thoroughly.

Pour into pie crust; refrigerate until completely chilled and serve.

Serves 6 to 8

MARLA GIBBS

MICHAEL Gross is well known as Steven Keaton, the father in the hit series *Family Ties*. On one of his last visits to *Hour,* he talked about his involvement as a spokesperson for ALS (Amyotrophic Lateral Sclerosis, often referred to as Lou Gehrig's disease) after he had made a movie of the week called *A Right to Die*. Michael always tries to go that extra mile and make a difference if he can. He once came on and brought his recipe for marinara sauce, which was simple yet tasty! Michael says the key is: Use as much garlic as you can, it never hurts!

♥ ♥   Michael's Marinara Sauce

1 yellow onion
4 large cloves garlic
2 tablespoons olive oil
Two 28-ounce cans Italian-style tomatoes
One 12-ounce can tomato paste
1 teaspoon freshly ground pepper
2 tablespoons dry or fresh basil
½ teaspoon salt
2 teaspoons garlic powder
1 pound thin spaghetti

Finely chop the onion and garlic cloves; sauté lightly in olive oil.

Add the Italian-style tomatoes (cut tomatoes as you add them) and the can of paste (with no additional water).

Add the pepper, basil, and salt and reduce heat. Cook on low heat (without a cover) for at least 2 hours.

Every ½ hour to 45 minutes check seasoning (this is when Michael usually adds garlic powder).

Note: The key is in the seasoning and in simmering for 2 hours (at least!).

Serves 4 (covers 1 pound spaghetti)

MICHAEL GROSS

CHRISTOPHER Hewett has had a varied career spanning over half a century. He was a child actor from age 6½, a member of England's most distinguished legitimate theater companies, a film actor remembered in movies like *The Producers,* a stage director, and a TV actor seen on *Fantasy Island* and presently *Mr. Belvedere.* He describes his role in *Mr. Belvedere* as that of "domestic engineer." He showed me that he was capable of cooking in real life with his recipes for lamb—Herbed Leg of Lamb—and for dessert—be still my heart—Chocolate Pots de Crème.

♥ ♥   **Herbed Leg of Lamb**

One 4½–5½-pound leg of lamb
1 clove garlic, peeled and halved
1 teaspoon Coleman's English Mustard
1 teaspoon salt
1 teaspoon pepper
½ teaspoon thyme
¼ teaspoon crushed rosemary leaves
1 tablespoon lemon juice
½ cup flour
Mint sauce or red currant jelly (optional)

Rub surfaces of the lamb with garlic. Mix the mustard with salt, pepper, thyme, rosemary, and lemon juice.

Spread and pack herb mixture on surface of the roast. Place roast on metal rack of the roasting dish.

Cover with aluminium foil tent and cook at 325° for 25 minutes per pound. Remove meat to a platter and skim off excess fat and juices.

Dissolve the flour in a small amount of cold water. Pour the juices into small saucepan, cook on high for 15 to 20 minutes and serve the herbed sauce with the meat.

Add mint sauce or red currant jelly if desired on the side.

Serves 8 to 10

CHRISTOPHER HEWETT

Chocolate Pots de Crème

     12 ounces semisweet chocolate (Ghirardelli or Baker's)
     ½ teaspoon salt
     1½ teaspoon vanilla
     1½ cups cream or half-and-half
      6 egg yolks

Cut chocolate squares in quarters.

Place chocolate, salt, and vanilla in blender.

Heat cream to boiling. Pour over chocolate. Blend 30 seconds. Pour in egg yolks. Blend 15 to 20 seconds. Pour into demitasse cups or pot de crème cups. Chill 4 hours *(can be frozen)*.

Serve with whipped cream. *(I don't sweeten this, but it's strictly a matter of taste.)*

Variation

Add 1½ tablespoons instant coffee for mocha—or some rum.

Serves 8 to 10

CHRISTOPHER HEWETT

TELMA Hopkins was a member of Dawn with Tony Orlando and more recently Nell Carter's sidekick on *Gimme a Break*. She and Nell Carter are such fun together. When Nell was a co-host, Telma came on to make a simple Italian Tomato Salad and then a holiday special from her childhood memories—*Yam Slam Pie!*

♥ ♥   # Italian Tomato Salad

      8 Italian plum tomatoes, quartered
      1 red onion, cut in chunks
      6 mushrooms, quartered (optional)
      1 tablespoon Parmesan cheese

1 tablespoon Romano cheese
  Salt-free vegetable seasoning (Vegit, Mrs. Dash)
2 tablespoons olive or other vegetable oil

Place tomatoes in a wide, shallow bowl. Add onion and mushrooms, if desired. Sprinkle with cheeses and seasoning. Drizzle with oil.

Serves 6

TELMA HOPKINS

Yam Slam Pie

4 medium yams
½ stick (4 tablespoons) butter
½ teaspoon lemon extract
½ teaspoon vanilla extract
3 medium eggs, slightly beaten
½ teaspoon nutmeg
½ teaspoon cinnamon
2½ cups sugar
6 ounces Pet evaporated milk
one 9-inch deep-dish pie crust

Preheat oven to 325°.
Boil the yams in a pot until fork tender (approximately 40 minutes). Rinse with cold water and peel. Transfer to a mixing bowl immediately. Mash yams together with the butter. Add the extracts and then the eggs. Next add the nutmeg, cinnamon, and sugar. Finally add the milk and mix thoroughly. Pour into a pie crust and bake for 1¼ hours (until pie is completely set).

Serves 6 to 8

TELMA HOPKINS

ANNA **Maria Horsford** was a producer for PBS, acted in movies like *St. Elmo's Fire* and *Class,* and starred in television pilots before she landed the role as Sherman Hemsley's surly daughter Thelma in the comedy series *Amen.* Even though *Amen* keeps her busy, she is still utilizing her producing talents through her involvement with Black Women in the Theater. She came on to make Salmon Croquettes that were among the best I've ever tasted!

♥ Salmon Croquettes with Béchamel Sauce

One 16-ounce can salmon, cleaned and boned
  ¼ cup chopped onion
  ¼ cup chopped green pepper
  ¼ teaspoon thyme
  ¼ teaspoon oregano
  ⅛ teaspoon garlic powder
  Salt and pepper to taste
  2 eggs, beaten
  3 tablespoons breadcrumbs
  ½ cup vegetable oil (for frying)
  1 cup flour (on plate for dredging)
  Béchamel Sauce (recipe follows)

Place salmon in large mixing bowl. Add onion, green pepper, and seasonings. Mix well. Add eggs, then breadcrumbs. Form mixture into small patties. Heat oil in heavy skillet. Dip patties into flour; shake off excess flour. Fry 2 to 3 minutes per side, until golden brown. Serve with Béchamel Sauce.

Béchamel Sauce

  4 tablespoons butter
  4 tablespoons flour
  1 cup milk

1 cup chicken broth
Salt and pepper to taste

Melt the butter in a saucepan over medium heat. Add flour to hot butter to make a paste; remove from heat and cool. Heat milk and broth together; gradually add to cooled flour mixture. Return to low heat and cook for 15 minutes. Stir often. Season with salt and pepper.

Serves 4

ANNA MARIA HORSFORD

M ARK Hudson is a member of the famous Hudson Brothers Trio—and was more recently Joan Rivers's sidekick on *The Late Show*. He made what he calls an Italian Steak with Mark's Salad and of course, it's hard to go wrong with such a classic dish.

Italian Steak

1 Porterhouse steak (¾ pound)
1 clove garlic, sliced
Fresh ground pepper (to taste)
¼ cup olive oil
4 tablespoons butter
2 tablespoons whole black peppercorns
2 tablespoons flour

Stud steak with 4 slices of garlic, using a knife to pierce the meat. Grind the pepper on both sides of the steak. Let the meat sit for ½ hour.

Heat oil and butter to a high temperature. Add whole peppercorns, then the steak (carefully, to avoid splattering), and cook over high heat for 2 to 3 minutes per side. Serve with sauce made by pouring off excess oil from pan, leaving peppercorns and ¼ cup of pan drippings. Stir in flour until smooth.

Serves 2 to 3

MARK HUDSON

Mark's Salad

  1 head iceberg lettuce, cut up
 ½ slice Maui sweet onion
  6 hard-boiled eggs (yolks only), whole
  8 ounces buffalo mozzarella, sliced
  2 tablespoons chopped basil
    Italian dressing to taste

Combine all ingredients. Toss with dressing.

Serves 6

MARK HUDSON

JACKEE was first a history teacher and then a stage actress before you knew her as Lily Masin on the daytime soap *Another World.* Today, she's the "spice in the pot"—as the lovable Sandra on *227,* a role that won her an Emmy earlier this year. One of TV's hottest performers, Jackee's offstage personality is good-hearted and charming, and she's still funny and sexy like Sandra!

♥ ## Jackee's Quick Vegetarian Delight

  1 cup margarine
  2 tablespoons olive oil
  6 ears of corn or 2 cups frozen
  3 zucchini squash, sliced into round pieces
  1 green pepper, sliced
  1 large tomato, wedged
  1 tablespoon garlic salt
    Salt and pepper to taste

Melt margarine with oil in skillet. Sauté husked corn off the cob for 10 to 15 minutes.
  Add zucchini and green pepper. Cover and simmer for 10 minutes.
  Add tomato. Cover and simmer for 5 minutes more.
  Season with garlic salt and salt and pepper.
  Serve over rice.

Serves 6

JACKEE

JOANNA Kerns is the star of *Growing Pains.* She had some personal and professional growing pains herself before this role. She often lived in the shadow of her sister, Olympic swimming star Donna de Varona. Joanna, a nationally ranked gymnast, was knocked out of competing in the 1970 World Games when she suffered a knee injury.

Today her career and talent as an actress is well established. She plays a mother who returns to her career as a journalist after rearing three children on *Growing Pains.* In real life, she is the mother of one daughter, Ashley, who's nine. And even though the scallops in her recipe are not cooked, her daughter Ashley likes this meal because it doesn't taste fishy!

♥ ♥   **Fiesta Scallops**

  1 pound medium scallops
½ cup lemon juice
  4 teaspoons instant minced onion
  1 teaspoon chili powder
  1 diced tomato
  4 teaspoons parsley flakes
  4 teaspoons oil

Combine scallops, lemon juice, onion, and chili powder. Chill 4 to 5 hours. Drain and toss with tomato, parsley flakes, and oil.

Serves 4

JOANNA KERNS

Someone's in the kitchen with Dinah—and it's football great Lyle Alzado, who traded in his football pads for an apron, with his recipe for Vegetables Lo Mein.

Frank's Place's Tim and Daphne Maxwell Reid invite the chef from the show, Don Yesso, on to make some Cajun food.

Teri Austin (*Knots Landing*) gets two thumbs up from Siskel & Ebert for her Angel Hair Pasta with Tomatoes and Feta.

No wonder Lynn Redgrave keeps her weight off—she's still so careful about measuring everything.

The hardest part for Jill St. John, who has a great cookbook herself, was getting the apron on — once we got past that, the pesto was irresistible. . . .

So, Joan, what is it? You're having another baby, David's not coming back, and you'd like *me* as your co-host???

Abby Dalton (*Falcon Crest*) and I chuckle as we watch Richard Simmons, silenced by his mother, Shirley Simmons.

Knowing what I know about *Dynasty*'s Adam Carrington, played by Gordon Thomson, I'm not sure I was willing even to taste his Spanish Soup.

Joan Fontaine, legendary actress and Cordon Bleu chef, joined me and made Poulet Orientale.

Charlton Heston and I watch Danny Pintauro (*Who's the Boss?*) make a Jell-O Surprise—that seems to have even Moses baffled!

Howie Mandel, also known as Dr. Fiscus, says that all food handlers should wear this, as Philip Charles MacKenzie (*Brothers*) and his wife, Linda Carlson, laugh along with me.

Rita Moreno has an Oscar, a Tony, an Emmy, and a Grammy, *and* a great recipe for "Picadillo" (Cubano).

I decided to let "Mr. Belvedere" get a chance to see what it feels like to be waited on. . . . Christopher Hewett made an Herbed Leg of Lamb and a dessert you won't forget.

Come on, Dr. Buscaglia . . . let's get it over with—I know we have to hug before we start cooking!

"Are you *sure* this is the right consistency for eggs?" ABC correspondent Sam Donaldson grills Brian Bonsall (*Family Ties*).

Dallas's Steve Kanaly and I are checking out Charo's recipe for quesadillas in our first cookbook. . . . This time she topped it with Fish Charo with Hollandaise Sauce.

Comedienne Samantha Fox kept David Brenner and me laughing—until we tasted her Linguine and Shrimp Puttanesca. . . .

"Now, Gary, this is serious—you've got to peel and chop the onions just right. . . ." For what? John Davidson's Peanut Sauce, to be used as a salad dressing or on chicken, beef, or lamb. Now that's serious!

Marla Gibbs (227) shows new mama Pamela Bellwood (*Dynasty*) how to make a meal that's healthy and quick (Stir-Fried Shrimp and Vegetables).

Danny Glover's using a lethal weapon to pound that boneless chicken breast for Chicken à la Tiffany made by *Small Wonder*'s Tiffany Brissette.

"Is salami and eggs better than sex?" Is Alan King actually asking Ana Alicia's (*Falcon Crest*) dog?

Alaina Reed (227) is the first guest who entered on wheels . . .

. . . and then made some collard greens and cornbread for Debbie Reynolds, Carrie Fisher, and Todd Fisher.

Jean Nidetch, a legend among weight watchers for twenty-five years, continues to sing the praises of good food!

Tommy Lasorda hugs Carol Lawrence and says, "I took a plate of Linguine with Clam Sauce, looked it right in the eye, and said, 'Who's stronger, you or me?' And the little clam looked right back at me and said, 'Linguine with Clam Sauce.'"

Night Court's John Larroquette joined Ali MacGraw and me for some Creole cooking—"but first," he said, "that smoking jacket's gotta go!"

Chef Tell takes us through the "perfect" meal — with . . . Nancy Sinatra . . .

. . . Johnny Mathis . . .

. . . and Dixie Carter.

Propmaster Chris Circosta and I talk through some of the plans for cooking demonstrations.

Trying out some of the *Hour Magazine* "Family" recipes backstage: (left to right) Maureen Poon-Fear, Catherine Pomponio, Carolyn DeRiggi, Gary Collins, Stephanie Modory, Kevin Fortson, Carol Uchita, Morris Abraham, Yvonne Alvarez, Martin Berman, and Chris Circosta.

Bert Greene always kept me in touch with one of the most important things in life . . . laughter.

H E'S a successful producer, actor, humanitarian, and of course, one of America's best-loved comedians. **Alan King** has a tremendous appetite for life which he shares in his latest book, *Is Salami and Eggs Better Than Sex?* In the book, he reminisces about people he's eaten with and those he's cooked for—and he's actually known for making his dinner parties into a real production!

He made his visit to *Hour* a production—filled with anecdotes à la King as only *he* could deliver!

Veal à la King

6 slices veal scallops, pounded
Salt and pepper
Flour
3 eggs, beaten
Seasoned breadcrumbs
1 tablespoon olive oil
2 tablespoons clarified butter (can use regular)
Lemon

Pound veal thin. Season with salt and pepper.
Dip in flour, shake off excess; dip in egg, then in breadcrumbs.
Heat oil and butter in skillet. Sauté quickly, approximately 4 minutes total. Squeeze lemon over scallops and serve.

Optional

Top cooked veal with 1 slice prosciutto ham, then sliced mozzarella or Swiss cheese. Place under broiler for 30 seconds. Serve.

Serves 4 to 6

ALAN KING

♥ ♥ ## Sautéed Peppers

1 large green bell pepper
1 large yellow bell pepper
1 large red bell pepper
1 large Spanish onion, sliced

1 tablespoon olive oil
2 tablespoons clarified butter (can use regular)
2 cloves garlic, minced
  Salt
  Pepper
  Hot pepper flakes

Slice peppers into strips. Heat oil and butter in pan.
Add peppers and onion. Sauté over high heat 3 to 4 minutes.
Add garlic, salt, pepper, and hot pepper flakes.
Continue to cook an additional 3 to 4 minutes. Serve with veal.

Serves 2 to 4

ALAN KING

Reprinted by permission of Alan King from *Is Salami and Eggs Better Than Sex?* copyright © 1985 by Alan King Productions, Inc., and Mimi Sheraton. Published by Little, Brown & Co.

PAUL **Kreppel** plays Sonny Mann on *It's a Living*—he's everyone's favorite sleazy lounge singer. And he came to the *Hour Magazine* kitchen and made a quick, healthy—a consistent theme!—Pasta Salad.

 ## Pasta Salad

Cut up your favorite vegetables into bite-sized pieces. Use vegetables such as tomatoes, broccoli, zucchini, bell peppers, mushrooms, and olives.

Marinate in Italian salad dressing for 1 hour. Add to cooked, drained corkscrew pasta (rotelle) and mix well.

This recipe can be made in any quantity of servings you need.

Quick and easy, this recipe is ideal for barbecues and picnics.

PAUL KREPPEL

N*IGHT COURT'S* **Dan Fielding** earned actor John Larroquette three Emmys. The character is arrogant but the actor is humble and painfully honest. Since 1981, he's been recovering from alcoholism and his openness about his struggle is aimed at helping others who may need to get help. Besides his personal work with recovering alcoholics in hospitals and rehabilitation wards, he works in theater and is writing fiction and drama. He brought a recipe from New Orleans, where he grew up in his grandparents' home on the outskirts of the French Quarter.

♥ ## Grillades and Grits

The old-time New Orleans version of smothered steak—veal or beef round pounded out thin, browned in hot fat, then slowly cooked with onions and fresh tomatoes. Grillades are always served with grits to soak up the rich natural gravy. They make a hearty inexpensive supper or a grand old-fashioned Sunday breakfast.

1¼–1¾- pound round of veal or beef
2 teaspoons salt
1 teaspoon freshly ground black pepper
⅛ teaspoon cayenne
1 tablespoon finely minced garlic
2 tablespoons flour
1½ tablespoons lard
1 cup chopped onion
1 large ripe Creole (beefsteak, Jersey) tomato, coarsely chopped
1 cup water, more if necessary
2½–3 cups cooked grits

Trim all the fat off the meat and remove any bones. Cut into pieces about 2 inches square and pound out with a mallet to about 4 inches square. Rub the salt, black pepper, cayenne, and garlic into the pieces of meat on both sides, then rub in the flour.

In a large heavy skillet or sauté pan, melt the lard over medium heat and brown the grillades well on both sides. Lower the heat and add the onion, tomato, and water. Bring to a simmer, cover loosely, and cook over low heat for about 30 minutes, uncovering to turn the meat over every 10 minutes. A rich brown gravy will form during cooking; if it appears too thick, add water a little bit at a time.

When the meat is cooked, remove it to a heated platter and place in a preheated 200° oven to keep warm. Prepare the grits according to package directions. Just before serving, reheat the gravy in the skillet, then pour it over both the meat and the grits.

Serves 4 to 6

JOHN LARROQUETTE

♥ ♥   **Old-Fashioned Soaked Salad**

An old-time home favorite. The salad is dressed, tossed, then refrigerated for several hours to let the greens and tomatoes soak up the dressing. The greens should be quite soft and look a trifle wilted. It is traditional to use two types of greens and medium-ripe tomatoes in this salad.

> 2 heads of lettuce (romaine, Boston, curly top, iceberg)
> 2 pounds medium-ripe Creole (beefsteak, Jersey) tomatoes

Dressing

> 6 tablespoons olive oil
> 1 tablespoon white wine vinegar
> 1 tablespoon fresh lemon juice
> ½ teaspoon salt
> ½ teaspoon dried basil or 1 teaspoon minced fresh basil
> ¼ teaspoon freshly ground black pepper
> ⅛ teaspoon sugar
> 1 teaspoon finely minced garlic
> 1 tablespoon finely minced fresh parsley

Wash and dry the lettuces. Wash the tomatoes, pare off the ends, and cut into chunks.

Put the lettuce and tomatoes into a large stainless-steel or porcelain bowl.

Combine the dressing ingredients in a small bowl and mix well with a wire whisk or a fork. Pour over the salad and toss to mix thoroughly. (It's all right to bruise the chunks of tomato a bit; their juice is an important part of the dressing. Just don't mash them.) Cover the bowl with plastic wrap and refrigerate for at least 3 hours.

To serve, use small dessert bowls or deep salad dishes and spoon about 2 tablespoons of the liquid from the bottom of the salad bowl over each portion.

Serves 10 to 12

JOHN LARROQUETTE

TOMMY Lasorda loves baseball. For thirty-six years he has worked for the Dodgers, as a player, scout, coach, and manager. And he's surely one of baseball's most successful and controversial managers. He says that he loves his job and the only thing he doesn't like about it is losing, since he's a bad loser. And winning and losing, says Tommy, who now owns a restaurant in Los Angeles (TOMMY LASORDA'S RIBS AND PASTA), affects his appetite. "When we win, I'm so happy I eat a lot. When we lose, I'm so depressed I eat a lot. And when we're rained out, I'm so disappointed I eat a lot." Eat a lot of Lasorda's Linguine—you'll love it!

Lasorda's Linguine
(With an assist from Carol Lawrence)

¼ pound (1 stick) butter
4 cloves garlic, minced
  Four 6½-ounce cans chopped clams, liquid reserved
½ cup minced parsley
¼ cup chopped walnuts
  Salt and pepper
1 pound cooked linguine
  Grated Parmesan cheese

Heat butter in a large skillet.
  Add garlic; cook until golden *(take care not to burn)*. Add clams and cook for 2 minutes more.
  Add parsley. Gradually add reserved clam juice until sauce is desired thickness. Add walnuts. Season with salt and pepper. Cook an additional 2 minutes.
  Toss with hot cooked linguine. Top with grated cheese and serve immediately.

Serves 4

TOMMY LASORDA

PHILIP Charles Mackenzie played the flamboyant and lovable Donald Maltby in the Showtime pay-cable series *Brothers* and is married to *Newhart*'s Linda Carlson. Philip told us that he's the primary cook in the family and he brought recipes for Chicken Piccata and Arugula Salad.

Chicken Piccata

1 tablespoon vegetable oil
5 tablespoons sweet butter
3 whole chicken breasts, filleted
    Salt and freshly ground pepper
    Juice of 1 lemon
3 tablespoons chopped parsley
1 lemon, thinly sliced

Heat oil and 3 tablespoons butter in a skillet over medium-high heat. When butter foam subsides, sauté fillets *briefly* on both sides (2 minutes tops).
Remove fillets to warm platter. Salt and pepper.
Add lemon juice to skillet; reduce heat to medium, scraping residue from bottom of pan, adding 1 to 2 tablespoons water, if necessary.
Add parsley and remaining 2 tablespoons butter to the cooking juices. Stir; lower heat to low; add fillets; turn quickly to coat.
Transfer to warm serving platter. Pour juices over; garnish with lemon slices.

Serves 4 to 6

PHILIP CHARLES MACKENZIE

♥ Arugula Salad

4 bunches arugula leaves
2 sweet red peppers, diced
½ cup gorgonzola cheese, crumbled

2 tablespoons red wine vinegar
6 tablespoons olive oil

Place arugula leaves in bowl.
Top with red peppers and cheese.
Toss with vinegar and oil.

Serves 2 to 4

LINDA CARLSON

YOU know **Edie McClurg** as Mrs. Poole on *Valerie's Family*. And from her character, you'd assume that she feels quite at home in the kitchen. She visited *Hour*'s kitchen and brought an unusual recipe—for Indian Chaputi—which are terrific pancakes!

 # Indian Chaputi

1 cup cold water
2 cups whole wheat flour
Butter
Honey

Add water to flour; blend with pastry blade. Form flour mixture into small meatball-size balls. Flour large cutting board. Roll flour balls into round 8-inch (approximately), thin pancakes.

Heat the griddle. Quickly cook pancakes on both sides. Transfer to the gas burner on the stove over high heat. Turn quickly.

Butter each pancake, drizzle with honey. Roll them into crepes.

Makes about 18 pancakes.

EDIE MCCLURG

H E played Ted Capwell on the daytime soap opera *Santa Barbara*. But off camera, **Todd McKee** is unlike his married character and seems to be a confirmed bachelor.

He shares a house with four friends and it seems that his life-style includes lots of parties. So he brought along a recipe for guacamole which is great for dips.

Seafood Guacamole à la *Santa Barbara*

     5 avocados
     2 cloves garlic
     1 tomato
     ½ onion
     ½ bell pepper
     1½ cups cooked baby shrimp
     ½ cup sour cream
        Salt and pepper
        Dash hot sauce
        Skin and juice of 1 lemon

Peel avocado with knife. Cut in half and remove pit. Put pit into a dip bowl and cut the rest of the avocados into a mixing bowl.

Mash all the avocados with a fork until the mixture looks smooth and not too lumpy.

Peel skin from garlic cloves and put into garlic crusher; add to avocados.

Finely chop the tomato and add to avocados.

Peel the onion and chop finely; add to avocados (should be in small pieces).

Cut the bell pepper up into small pieces and add to the avocados.

Cut up the baby shrimp into halves or thirds and add to dip. Reserve some shrimp to garnish the dip when finished.

Add 2 tablespoons sour cream to avocados and mix all ingredients together. Now add salt, pepper, and hot sauce to taste; mix together. Add squeeze of lemon.

Leaving the pit of 1 avocado in the dip bowl, pour the guacamole into the dip bowl. Garnish around the edges with the baby shrimp to make it pretty, and top it off with a spoonful of sour cream. You can cut small pieces of skin from the lemon to use as decoration around the bowl.

Make-It-Easy Tip: The reason the pit is left in the bottom and lemon juice is added is to keep the dip from going brown.

Serves 4

                                                          TODD McKEE

A S most of you know, **Mary Ann Mobley** is my wife. It's hard to believe that this year we celebrated her thirtieth anniversary of winning the Miss America pageant as co-hosts of that gala event. In addition to guesting on *Falcon Crest* this year, she continues to stay involved with many charitable organizations. Her latest activity is scuba diving. What's really a miracle to me is that she still has time to cook for us, and she's great at it too. This is an Italian dish, but everything Mary Ann cooks ends up having a down-home flavor to it!

♥ Veal Piccata

  8 medium scallops or medallions of white veal, pounded
    thin
    Flour Mixture for dredging
  2 tablespoons olive oil
  4 tablespoons sweet butter
  2 tablespoons minced shallots
  4 tablespoons lemon juice, freshly squeezed
  ¼ cup white wine or veal stock
  2 tablespoons capers
  8 lemon slices for garnish
  2 tablespoons chopped parsley

Flour Mixture

  1 cup white flour
  1 tablespoon salt
  1 tablespoon white pepper
  1 tablespoon paprika

Mix all flour mixture ingredients together and place on a large, flat platter.
    Place scallops in flour mixture to coat each side; shake off excess. Heat oil and butter in a large heavy skillet. Add shallots. Sauté for 1 minute. Add veal; sauté 2 to 3 minutes until lightly browned. Remove to a warm serving platter. Add lemon juice, wine, and capers. Increase heat. Stir and scrape bottom of skillet until sauce thickens. Pour sauce over veal. Garnish with lemon slices and sprinkle with parsley.

Note: Breast of chicken or turkey may be substituted for veal.

Serves 4

MARY ANN MOBLEY

RITA Moreno has been described as "electric," "dynamic," "exuberant," and the list goes on. She came to the United States from Puerto Rico when she was very young and always knew that someday she'd be a star. Beginning her professional career at thirteen, she pursued her dreams and is in the record book for having won all four major show business awards: the Oscar, the Emmy, the Grammy, and the Tony. Her astounding range of abilities doesn't stop outside the kitchen either—here's her recipes for "Picadillo" (Cubano) and Chicken Breasts with Julienne Vegetables.

♥ ## "Picadillo" (Cubano)

¼ cup annatto oil
1 large green bell pepper, seeded and finely chopped
3 cloves garlic, finely chopped
¾ pound ground beef
2 large tomatoes, peeled and chopped (should make 2 cups)
Cumin to taste
½ cup seedless raisins
¼ cup pimento-stuffed green olives/rounds/spiced
1 tablespoon capers
1 large onion, finely chopped
1 small red pepper, chopped (optional)
¼ pound ground pork
Pepper to taste

Put all ingredients in a big skillet and cook until done. Serve over white rice.

Serves 4

RITA MORENO

♥ ## Chicken Breasts with Julienne Vegetables

4 large boneless and skinless chicken breast halves (1½ pounds)
1 small carrot, cut in julienne strips
1 small zucchini, cut in julienne strips
2 tablespoons thinly sliced green onion

¼ teaspoon dried thyme leaves
　2 tablespoons unsalted butter or margarine
One 10½-ounce can Campbell's Low Sodium Cream of
　　　Mushroom Soup
　1 tablespoon chopped parsley

Flatten chicken breasts on cutting board.

Holding sharp knife horizontally, cut a pocket in each breast. Stuff breasts with carrot, zucchini, and onion; sprinkle with thyme. Press edges of pocket together.

In a 10-inch skillet over medium heat, cook chicken breasts in hot butter until browned on both sides.

Stir in soup; cover. Reduce heat; simmer 30 minutes, or until chicken is done.

To serve: Slice chicken breasts diagonally. Spoon sauce into serving plate. Arrange chicken slices over sauce. Sprinkle with parsley.

Serves 4.

RITA MORENO

COUNTRY and pop singer **Gary Morris**, who was honored with an induction to the Country Music Hall of Fame's Walkaway of Stars, did a stint as an actor on the *Dynasty* spin-off *The Colbys*. The ex-college football star left his hometown of Nashville to play Wayne Masterson, a blind singer. Morris hoped that the show exposed his music to a wider audience, influencing them toward country music. He's a single parent raising his son Sam, so I know his recipe for Enchiladas Verdes really works!

　　　　　　　　Enchiladas Verdes

Chili Verde

　2 pounds pork loin, cubed
　8 large Anaheim chilies, sliced (or other mild chili)
　4 jalapeño peppers, sliced
　2 onions, quartered
　4 tomatoes, quartered
　2 cloves garlic, minced
　　Salt and pepper to taste
　½ cup flour

Flour Tortillas

4 cups self-rising flour
1 tablespoon salt
1 tablespoon butter, softened
2 cups water (approximately)

Enchiladas

Flour tortillas
Chili Verde
3 tomatoes, diced
2 onions, diced
4 cups shredded cheddar cheese

Make chili verde: Brown pork in a skillet. Drain off fat.
Place in an 8-quart pot. Add remaining ingredients **except flour**. Cover with water.
Bring to a boil. Reduce heat to low. Cook for 3 hours.
Mix flour with enough water to make a paste. Add to chili and cook for 15 minutes more, or until chili has thickened.
Make flour tortillas: Fit food processor with pastry blade.
Add flour, salt, and butter and process gradually, adding water until dough has reached an elastic consistency.
Flour a large cutting board. Take a small amount of dough mixture and roll out into an 8-inch round thin shape.
Place in a hot skillet, *preferably cast iron.* Brown both sides and set aside.
Continue process until all of the dough is used. Makes 16 to 20 tortillas.
Assemble enchiladas: Butter a 9×12-inch glass baking dish.
Lay tortillas flat, adding a small amount of chili, tomato, onion, and cheese. Roll up; place seam side down in baking dish. Continue until dish is filled.
Top with additional Chili Verde and lots of cheese.
Bake in a 400° oven until hot and bubbly.
Serve immediately.

Serves 8 to 10

GARY MORRIS

Eggs in a Nest

White bread
Butter
Eggs

Cut a hole in the middle of a bread slice, using a cookie cutter.

Place bread in buttered frying pan or griddle. Crack egg into hole in center of bread. Grill bread and egg. Turn over and grill other side. The egg will grill with the bread.

Serves 3

JENNY O'HARA

Apple Phyllo Tart

12 leaves phyllo dough
1 pound unsalted butter, melted
1 cup sugar
5 ounces Grand Marnier or orange juice concentrate
6 medium Granny Smith apples, cored and thinly sliced

Defrost phyllo leaves and cover with a damp towel for 10 minutes.

Lay 1 phyllo leaf in a 14-inch jelly-roll pan (nonstick). Brush with butter; sprinkle with 1 tablespoon sugar and 1 teaspoon Grand Marnier. Repeat for 6 layers.

Place 1 layer of sliced apples on top of sixth layer. Brush with butter and sprinkle with sugar and liqueur.

Continue layering with remaining ingredients.

Bake in preheated 425° oven for 35 to 40 minutes.

Serve warm with whipped cream or vanilla ice cream.

Serves 8 to 10

JENNY O'HARA

THAAO Penghlis was a native of Sydney (his Greek family migrated to Australia) where he was working as the vice-consulate to Greece. Somehow, he ended up in California, appeared in films like *Altered States,* TV soaps like *General Hospital,* and visited us when he was Count Tony DiMeara on *Days of Our Lives.*

He gave us an authentic recipe for Strava, an exclusive Kastellorizian sweet that derives its name from the oblique angle on which it is cut. It is considered to be the ultimate in Kastellorizian sweets and is therefore only made for weddings and name days.

Strava

Syrup

3 pounds honey
1 cup water
1 cup sugar

Pastry

1 cup olive oil
2 pounds plain flour
Water

Filling

1 pound walnut pieces
1 cup shredded coconut
1 level teaspoon each ground cloves, nutmeg, and cinnamon
1 pound almond pieces

1 cup sugar
    Peanut oil for deep frying

Bring the syrup ingredients to a boil. Set aside to cool. Make pastry: Rub oil
into flour and add sufficient water to make a soft dough. Knead for at least 10
minutes until dough is smooth in texture and whitish in color. Divide into 3
sections. Roll out fairly thinly. Brush with olive oil. Combine filling ingredients.
Sprinkle pastry all over with nut-coconut filling and roll up firmly. Cut on oblique
lines at approximately 3-inch intervals.

Heat oil and cook pastry for about 12 minutes. Place in colander to drain off
surplus oil. Place strava in honey mixture and leave for 10 minutes.

Makes 60 strava

THAAO PENGLIS

S HE shared classrooms with actors Peter O'Toole and Albert Finney
at the Royal Academy of Dramatic Art and left England to visit her
friends in America. In New York, **Christina Pickles,** who you know best
as Nurse Helen from *St. Elsewhere,* thrived playing Broadway and off
Broadway and appearing in two soap operas.

She made an unusual salad and a spaghetti sauce in *Hour*'s kitchen.

♥   ## Prosciutto Ham and Peach Salad

    2 bunches Bibb lettuce, washed and torn
   ½ pound prosciutto ham, chopped
    2 large ripe peaches, peeled and sliced, or 3 canned
        peaches, sliced
   18 small pitted olives

Toss ingredients with mustard vinegar dressing.

Serves 4

CHRISTINA PICKLES

Christina Pickles's Spaghetti Sauce

   2 cups mushrooms, loosely chopped and cleaned
   2 cups tomatoes, chopped and peeled
1½ cups green pitted olives, chopped
   1 teaspoon fennel seed
   4 tablespoons olive oil
     Salt and pepper to taste

Combine all ingredients in saucepan.
Cook over medium heat until hot.
Pour over hot pasta.

Makes about 2 cups

CHRISTINA PICKLES

LYNN **Redgrave,** whose acting career began with her performance in the movie *Georgy Girl,* also starred in two TV series, *House Calls* and *Teachers Only.*
   Lately she's been a spokesperson for Weight Watchers and has hosted a videocassette called *Weight Watchers Magazine Guide to Dining and Cooking.* In it, Lynn advises dieters on how to order low-calorie meals when dining out and how to make imaginative and delicious meals at home. Here's one worth trying!

Pasta with Onion Sauce

⅓ cup olive oil, divided
   2 medium onions, cut in half lengthwise, thinly sliced
   3 cloves garlic, minced
   4 cups cooked small macaroni shells
   2 cups Boston lettuce leaves or chicory, torn into bite-size
     pieces
   1 ounce grated Parmesan or Romano cheese
   1 teaspoon chopped sage leaves (or herb or your choice)
     Freshly ground pepper to taste

In medium skillet over medium heat, heat 2 tablespoons oil.

Add onions and sauté until translucent. Add garlic; stir. Remove from burner; cool completely.

In a large serving bowl, toss onion-garlic mixture with remaining olive oil and all other ingredients.

Serves 2 to 4

LYNN REDGRAVE

A LAINA Reed, who has been playing Olivia the photographer on the award-winning *Sesame Street* for over ten years, is truly a fun-loving person! Her other featured role is as Rose, the good-hearted neighbor on *227* each week. Alaina, who lived in New Jersey with her two children, moved out to Los Angeles to do *227* and flies back to New York on her days off to act in *Sesame Street.* She says that she got her strong work ethic from her grandmother who taught her to "work hard and always go forward." That explains why she also released a children's video she co-produced and starred in called *Learning Can Be Fun.* Cooking can be fun, too, whenever I have guests like Alaina.

Collard Greens

½ pound salt pork, sliced
½ cup sugar
4 cloves garlic, minced
  Ground pepper
2 onions, chopped
2 large tablespoons shortening
2 bundles collard greens, cooked 40 minutes
2 bundles mustard greens, cooked 40 minutes
2 bundles turnip greens, cooked 40 minutes
1 bundle kale greens, cooked 30 minutes

Fill a large pot ¼ full of water and put it over medium heat on top of the stove. Toss in all the ingredients except for the greens. Let it "brew" while you wash the uncooked greens thoroughly and devein them (take the center stems out). Toss in the collard greens, then the mustard greens, then the turnip greens. The kale greens *must* go in last.

Let it cook "till it's done." The greens will make their own water, so don't worry about there not being enough in the pot. Collard greens taste their best when served with cornbread or hush puppies.

Serves 6 to 8

ALAINA REED

SUSAN **Ruttan** portrays Roxanne Melman, the secretary to Arnie Becker (played by Corbin Bernsen), in *L.A. Law*. Before acting herself, Susan was a casting director who had a clothing company with Joel Brooks *(My Sister Sam)*. Together they designed oversized jackets and shirts. Now her role on *L.A. Law* keeps her busy, but she always has time to make a great meal like this—Chicken Chili and Cheese Bread!

♥ ## Chicken Chili

            6 tablespoons olive oil
            1 onion, chopped
            5 cloves garlic, minced
            2 sweet red peppers, diced
            4 jalapeño peppers, minced
            3 tablespoons chili powder
       1½ teaspoons cumin powder
            1 teaspoon ground coriander
            1 tablespoon cinnamon
            6 chicken breasts, skinned, boned, and cubed
          16 ounces tomato puree
            8 ounces sliced olives
            1 cup beer or chicken broth
          ¼ cup grated unsweetened chocolate
             Grated cheddar cheese
             Avocado
             Sour cream

Heat 3 tablespoons olive oil in a large saucepan or Dutch oven. Add onion and garlic. Sauté 2 to 3 minutes. Add both peppers and continue to sauté for 10 minutes. Add chili powder, cumin, coriander, and cinnamon. Stir, then reduce heat.

Heat remaining 3 tablespoons olive oil in a skillet. Add chicken and cook quickly, until chicken turns white. Drain and add to saucepan. Add tomato puree, olives, and beer or broth. Add grated chocolate and mix well. Simmer for 15 to 20 minutes more. Serve. Garnish with grated cheese, avocado, and sour cream.

Serves 6

SUSAN RUTTAN

♥ Cheese Bread

1 loaf French bread
2 tablespoons olive oil
  Oregano to taste
¼ cup Parmesan cheese

Split loaf of bread lengthwise. Brush with olive oil and then sprinkle with oregano and Parmesan cheese. Put under the broiler for 2 to 3 minutes.

SUSAN RUTTAN

♥ ## Linguine Royale

½ cup sliced onion
½ cup sliced green pepper
1 tablespoon butter
8 large shrimps, peeled and deveined
1 cup sliced mushrooms
3 cups marinara sauce
¼ cup sherry or clam juice
8 ounces linguine, cooked

Sauté onions and green pepper in butter for 2 to 3 minutes. Add shrimps; sauté 2 to 3 minutes. Add mushrooms; sauté 1 minute. Add sauce and sherry and simmer for 10 minutes. Serve over the cooked linguine.

Serves 4

KAREN SALKIN

♥ ## Bavarian Cream Jell-O

1 4-ounce package Jell-O (strawberry or raspberry)
¼ cup sugar
1 cup boiling water
¾ cup orange juice
1 cup Dream Whip topping (or whipped cream)

Pour Jell-O and sugar into a mixing bowl. Add boiling water, stirring until Jell-O is completely dissolved. Add the orange juice. Refrigerate for approximately 1 hour, until Jell-O is just beginning to set. Fold in the whipped topping. Pour mixture into a ring mold. Refrigerate 3 to 4 hours, until completely set.

Serves 4

KAREN SALKIN

EMMA Samms, the English actress who came to fame on *General Hospital,* went on to become one of the leads of *Dynasty.* When she was only nine, her eight-year-old brother Jamie got sick and died of aplastic anemia. That event changed her life and is the reason Emma co-founded the Starlight Foundation, a charitable organization which grants wishes to critically, chronically, and terminally ill children. This past year she starred on *The Colbys* and when that show was canceled, she was asked to come back to play Fallon Carrington on *Dynasty,* where you can see her each week!

Quesadilla

    4 medium shrimp, cooked and chopped
    ¼ cup lime juice
    ¼ cup chopped cilantro
    2 tablespoons butter
    2 large flour tortillas
    ½ cup shredded white cheddar cheese
    2 tablespoons mild green chilies, chopped
    2 tablespoons chopped green onions
    2 tablespoons red chili salsa
    2 tablespoons sour cream
    2 tablespoons guacamole
    1 tablespoons chopped black olives

Marinate shrimp in lime juice and cilantro. Melt butter in 10″ sauté pan. Place one of the tortillas in pan. Top with half the cheese, the shrimp, green chilies, onions, and salsa, then the remaining cheese. Cook for 2 minutes (until underside is golden brown). Place second tortilla on top and flip the quesadilla over. Cook for an additional 2–3 minutes. Remove. Slice into wedges. Top with sour cream, guacamole, and olives.

Serves 2

EMMA SAMMS

WILLARD Scott from *The Today Show* is everybody's favorite weatherman. He's always so energetic and seems to bring excitement to everything he does. The last time he visited *Hour*'s kitchen, he had his very own cookbook called *Willard Scott's All American Cookbook* and made a breakfast meal, Puff Pastry, that you definitely should try yourself!

Puff Pastry

Pillsbury Rolled Dough Mix and whatever ingredients
   necessary per box
Grease or shortening

Prepare dough per package instructions. Cover with towel and allow to sit for 2 to 3 hours. Then refrigerate until the next day. (This destroys some, but not all, of the power of the yeast.)

On the second, day, dust board with flour and roll dough into paper-thin pieces.

Slice into strips 3 × 1½ inches.

Heat shortening in skillet until bubbles begin to form.

Toss a few strips of dough into the pan. In just seconds it will puff up like a balloon.

Turn gently with tongs, and allow to brown *very* lightly.

Quickly remove and put on platter lined with paper towels.

Variation

To make puffs extra tasty, open at one end with a knife and fill them with jam or some other goody.

WILLARD SCOTT

♥ ♥   Chicken in a Pot

One 4–5-pound chicken
3 white onions, sliced
4 stalks celery, chopped
1 jar pickling spices
16 ounces unfiltered apple juice
6 ounces Scotch

Wash chicken. Place in clay pot.
Add onions, celery, and pickling spices. Pour apple juice and Scotch over chicken.
Do not preheat oven. Set oven temperature at 400° and cook for 2 hours.
Serve over rice.
(Scotch cooks off, leaving no alcohol content.)

Serves 6

DOUG SHEEHAN

♥   Radicchio Salad with Raspberry Walnut Vinaigrette

1 small head radicchio lettuce
1 small head Belgian endive
1 small head butter lettuce
1 small head watercress
½ cup sliced mushrooms
½ cup sliced cucumbers

3 tablespoons crumbled goat cheese
Raspberry Walnut Vinaigrette (recipe follows)

Tear lettuces into bite-sized pieces.
Add mushrooms and cucumbers, and mix.
Top salad with goat cheese.
Add Raspberry Walnut Vinaigrette dressing and toss salad.

Serves 4

DOUG SHEEHAN

 ## Raspberry Walnut Vinaigrette

⅓ cup walnut oil
2 tablespoons raspberry vinegar
¼ teaspoon dried basil
Salt and pepper
3 tablespoons chopped walnuts

Mix together and pour over salad.

Makes about ½ cup

DOUG SHEEHAN

RICHARD Simmons, who had his own show focused on good health, diet, and exercise, certainly knows a lot about food. He's a great example of how much more energy we'd all have if we ate right! It's hard for Richard to be still and quiet for a minute!
His recipe for Shrimp and Chicken Jambalaya has everything healthy in it—including brown rice!

Shrimp and Chicken Jambalaya

½ cup chopped green bell pepper
2 cloves garlic, minced
½ cup chopped fresh parsley

⅔ cup chopped celery
2 cups chicken stock
One 16-ounce can tomatoes, chopped with juice
1 cup chopped scallions, white and green parts
1 teaspoon thyme
1 teaspoon oregano
1 bay leaf
1 tablespoon creole spice mixture
2 cups brown rice
1½ raw shrimp, peeled and cut in half
1½ pounds raw cubed chicken

Preheat oven to 350°.

Sauté peppers, garlic, parsley, and celery with ½ cup chicken stock for 5 minutes.

Add tomatoes with juice, rest of stock, and scallions.

Stir in thyme, oregano, bay leaf, and spice mixture. Stir in rice—reduce heat to simmer and cover—and cook 30 minutes.

Remove from stove, stir in shrimp and chicken, cover, and bake 10 to 12 minutes.

Serves 6

RICHARD SIMMONS

YAKOV Smirnoff is everybody's favorite Russian comic. He made Caviar Blinis and we invited his mother, who was sitting in the audience, for a taste test. She tasted it and then, very matter-of-factly stated (in Russian!), "Stick with comedy!"

Caviar Blinis

2 eggs, beaten lightly
1 cup milk
1 cup flour
1 tablespoon butter

1 cup sour cream
4 ounces caviar

Mix eggs, milk, and flour together to a thin consistency. Melt butter in a pan. Pour in pancake mixture. Cook 2 minutes per side. Place on a plate and fill with sour cream and caviar. Roll up. Top with additional sour cream and caviar.

Serves 2

YAKOV SMIRNOFF

J ILL St. John likes cooking as much as acting. She has been appearing on *Good Morning America* with her regular monthly cooking segments and writing a food column for *USA Weekly.* Her cookbook, *The Jill St. John Cookbook,* is a compilation of her extensive collection of recipes from her travels around the world on film locations. She also included recipes she calls "standby classics." The one she prepared in *Hour's* kitchen demands a food processor and it's a terrific great way to make a great Italian sauce and keep it for a few meals.

♥ ## Processor Pesto

2 cups fresh basil leaves
4 garlic cloves, minced
⅓ cup freshly grated Parmesan cheese
3 tablespoons pine nuts
½ cup olive oil
Salt to taste
1 pound hot cooked pasta such as spaghetti
Whole basil leaves for garnish

Place all ingredients, except the pasta and whole basil leaves for garnish, in the work bowl of a food processor that has been fitted with the steel blade. Process until you have a smooth paste.

Store in a glass jar covered with a thin layer of olive oil. Keeps a week or more, tightly sealed in the refrigerator.

To serve, bring to room temperature and place over hot pasta. (Allow 3 to 4 tablespoons pesto per serving.) Toss well. Garnish with whole basil leaves and serve with a bowl of freshly grated Parmesan cheese.

Serves 4 to 6

JILL ST. JOHN

Reprinted by permission of Jill St. John from *The Jill St. John Cookbook.* Copyright © 1987 by Jill St. John. Published by Random House, Inc., New York.

RICHARD Stahl portrays Howard Miller, the dry-witted cook, in *It's a Living.* Behind the scenes he actually was a cook for a short while at the Hotel Del Coronado outside of San Diego. When he visited us, he made an unusual dish that can be used as an entrée with a salad or a vegetable.

♥ ## Richard Stahl's Potato Volcanoes

    4 cups mashed potatoes
    ½ cup grated cheddar cheese
    ⅓ cup Mexican salsa or ketchup
    ½ cup bacon bits
    1 cup broccoli florets, blanched

In a round 8-inch baking pan, form potatoes in volcano shape.
Make a well at the top. Streak the sides of the potato mound with a fork.
Sprinkle with cheddar cheese and broil until golden brown.
Remove from oven. Pour salsa into well. Sprinkle with bacon bits.
Arrange broccoli florets around the base and serve.

Serves 4

RICHARD STAHL

♥ ♥   Barbara Stock's Tomato Basil Pasta

     4 tablespoons olive oil
   2–3 cloves garlic, minced
    10 tomatoes, peeled and seeded
       Salt and pepper to taste
     3 tablespoons chopped fresh basil
     1 pound angel hair or other thin pasta
       Freshly grated Parmesan cheese

Heat oil in a skillet and sauté garlic for 1 minute.

Add tomatoes and salt and pepper, and cook with cover on for 10 to 12 minutes, or until the tomatoes soften.

Stir in basil. Cook for an additional 5 minutes.

Serve over cooked pasta.

Top with grated cheese.

Serves 4

BARBARA STOCK

♥   Veal Milanese

     1 pound veal cutlets
    ½ cup olive oil
     2 eggs, beaten
     1 cup seasoned breadcrumbs
       Lemon slices

Tenderize veal until it's ¼ inch thick.

Heat oil in heavy skillet. Dip cutlets into egg mixture, then coat with breadcrumbs, shaking off the excess crumbs.

Fry in skillet until golden brown and remove to a warm platter.

Top with lemon slices.

Serves 4

BARBARA STOCK

♥ ♥   # Marinated Chicken

Marinating Mix

¼ cup dry sherry
1 tablespoon cornstarch
1 pinch celery salt
1 tablespoon soy sauce
1 pinch coriander
2 slices fresh ginger

1 pound skinned, boneless chicken breasts, sliced into narrow strips
3 tablespoons peanut oil, plus more for stir-frying
1 thin slice fresh ginger
2½ cups thinly sliced celery
½ cup diced sweet red peppers
1–2 cups chicken broth
¾ cup mushrooms
1 cup bean sprouts

Set the chicken strips in the Marinating Mix and set aside.

Put 3 tablespoons peanut oil into wok, then put wok over a high flame. Add a thin slice of ginger.

After the oil is hot, remove ginger slice; add marinated chicken. Brown quickly.

Remove browned chicken to separate plate. Add more oil. Toss in celery slices and red peppers; stir fast; add chicken broth and mushrooms. Cover wok and cook for 4 minutes, stirring occasionally.

Add chicken to wok with 1 cup bean sprouts; stir-fry quickly. Remove contents of wok with spoon and drain.

Serve on rice.

Serves 4

MARTHA SMITH

♥ Baked Bananas

4 bananas (not too ripe and cut in half lengthwise)
Juice of ½ orange (equivalent to ½ cup orange juice)
2 tablespoons brown sugar
½ teaspoon cinnamon
Kiwi slices

Preheat oven to 350°.
Butter a shallow baking dish and lay the bananas side by side, peeled.
Using mixer on medium speed, mix orange juice, brown sugar, and cinnamon and sprinkle this on top of the bananas.
Dot 1½ tablespoons butter onto bananas and bake for 15 minutes.
Serve garnished with kiwi slices.

Serves 4

MARTHA SMITH

MICHAEL Talbott, from *Miami Vice,* came on to prepare a "Miami" special meal. Recently Michael went on a weight-loss program and lost a significant amount of weight. I'm sure that now he'll only stick with his Miami Melon Chicken and leave the Key Lime Pie (which was great!) for his guests.

♥ ♥ Miami Melon Chicken

3 tablespoons oil
4 boneless chicken breasts, split
Salt and pepper to taste
1 tablespoon minced ginger
1 cup watermelon juice

Heat oil in skillet. Season chicken with salt and pepper. Sauté breasts in oil, 3 to 4 minutes each side. Add ginger and watermelon juice to pan. Reduce heat and simmer for an additional 5 minutes. Serve over brown rice.

Serves 4 to 6

MICHAEL TALBOTT

Key Lime Pie

4 egg yolks
One 16-ounce can sweetened condensed milk
¼ cup Key lime juice (or any lime juice)
One 9-inch premade graham cracker crust

Beat egg yolks into sweetened condensed milk. Add lime juice. Blend together and pour into crust. Refrigerate and chill until firm. Serve with whipped cream.

Serves 6 to 8

MICHAEL TALBOTT

GORDON Thomson plays Adam Carrington each week on *Dynasty*. Born in Canada, Gordon's early acting was in Canadian theater. When he came to America, he played in theater productions and then in a daytime soap, *Ryan's Hope,* for a short time. Gordon sees himself as totally different from his *Dynasty* character, and I can tell you there's none of Adam Carrington's evil lurking behind this man!

You can tell from the recipe he's a real garlic lover. Try this Spanish Soup—it probably can even cure a cold!

♥ ♥
Spanish Soup

5–6 cloves garlic, peeled and minced
3 Spanish onions, peeled and sliced
2–3 leeks, sliced
3 tablespoons oil
5 large tomatoes, peeled, seeded, and chopped
1 jar pickled red pepper or 1 red bell pepper, chopped
1 green pepper, chopped
8 cups water
2–3 cups minced cabbage
2–3 bay leaves
Salt to taste

1 teaspoon thyme
5–6 cloves
Peppercorns

Sauté garlic, onions, and leeks in oil in a large pot for 5 minutes.
Add tomatoes and peppers. Simmer for 25 minutes.
Add water and the rest of the ingredients and simmer for 1½ hours.

Bouillabaisse

½ pounds flaky white fish
6 shrimps
6 scallops
4 cups Spanish Soup

Combine ingredients and cook for 10 minutes.

Serves 6

GORDON THOMSON

B RENDA Vaccaro, who you know from movies like *Midnight Cowboy* and *Once Is Not Enough,* recently appeared in *Cookie* with actor Peter Falk. Brenda got her start in theater (she's earned three Tony nominations) before moving into film and television. She is without a doubt one of the funniest and most energetic guests we've had on the show.

When she co-hosted with me, she said that the greatest Italian sauce and meatballs were made by her mother, Christine, who owns a restaurant called MARIO'S in Dallas, Texas. So naturally, Brenda called her mother from the *Hour Magazine* kitchen and Christine dictated as Brenda and I made out-of-this-world meatballs!

Mario's Meatballs with Tomato Sauce (Christine Vaccaro)

2 tablespoons Crisco oil
6 slices decrusted bread
2 pounds chuck beef, ground once
4 eggs
Salt to taste

2 tablespoons chopped parsley
2 tablespoons sweet basil, cut with scissors
¾ cup Parmesan cheese
Mario's Tomato Sauce (recipe follows)

Slowly heat the oil in a skillet.

Place the decrusted bread in a bowl of cold water until soft. Remove bread and squeeze out excess water.

In a large bowl combine the ground chuck beef, eggs, salt, parsley, basil, bread, and cheese. Mix the ingredients with hands or a fork. Dip hands in cold water and roll 2-inch meatballs. Place the meatballs in the heated oil until browned on both sides and medium-rare inside.

Place meatballs in prepared tomato sauce and cook for 15 minutes.

BRENDA VACCARO

♥ ♥　　Mario's Tomato Sauce

2 tablespoons olive oil
1 cup chopped carrots
1 cup chopped celery
2 cups chopped onions
Salt to taste
Pepper to taste
1 large can Hunt's pear-shaped tomatoes, diced
3 cans Hunt's pureed tomatoes
1 teaspoon sugar
4 cloves garlic, diced
½ cup fresh sweet basil leaves

Cover the bottom of a skillet with olive oil and heat. Add carrots, celery, onions, salt, and pepper to the heated oil.

Combine the diced pear-shaped tomatoes and pureed tomatoes in a large pot. Add sugar, garlic, basil, and salt and pepper to taste. Stir on low flame. Add skillet mix and continue to heat for 30 minutes. Pour the heated tomato sauce into a colander to strain the vegetables.

Serves 4 to 5 (15 to 17 meatballs)

BRENDA VACCARO

Chocolate Mousse

1 pint whipping cream
3 tablespoon's Hershey's unsweetened cocoa
1 pint chocolate fudge sauce (Baskin-Robbins sells it. Used for hot fudge sundaes. Chocolate syrup will NOT do.) Sauce should be cooled.
Jigger of rum (optional)
Shavings of unsweetened or bittersweet chocolate

Whip cream until it is stiff.
Sift cocoa over whipped cream and fold into cream.
Fold fudge sauce into whipped cream and blend until smooth.
Fold rum into cream mixture. Spoon mixture into sherbert glasses. Refrigerate.
Just before serving, top with shaved chocolate.

Serves at least 8

ABIGAIL VAN BUREN

♥ Judge Wapner's Au Gratin Potatoes

4 medium-sized potatoes
Margarine
Nutmeg
1 large onion
Sharp cheddar cheese
Grated Parmesan cheese

Slice potatoes in a Cuisinart.

Parboil them for 3 minutes. Place in a pan smeared with margarine. Sprinkle nutmeg on potatoes, add sliced onion, add ¼ pound grated cheddar cheese, and top with Parmesan.

Bake 40 minutes at 350°.

Serves 4

JUDGE WAPNER

Chicken Prince of Wales

The pretty nineteenth-century town of Niagara-on-the-Lake sits on the shores of Lake Ontario at the mouth of the Niagara River. From 1792 to 1796, it was the capital of Upper Canada. Fudge is still made on marble slabs, luscious jam is created from local fruit, and the Prince of Wales Hotel was host to royalty as far back as 1901.

    4 whole chicken breasts, boned, cut in half, and flattened
      with a mallet
    Salt
    Pepper
    1 cup all-purpose flour
    4 eggs, beaten
    1 cup pecans or hazelnuts, coarsely chopped
    ¼ cup butter
    2 tablespoons vegetable oil

Sauce

    2 tablespoons butter
    2 teaspoons finely chopped shallots
    1 teaspoon finely chopped garlic
    1 tablespoon Dijon mustard
    ¼ cup medium dry white wine
    2 cups whipping cream
    Salt
    Pepper

    Season chicken breasts with salt and pepper, dredge lightly in flour, then dip into beaten eggs. Dip into coarsely chopped hazelnuts and press in with wooden spoon.

In a frying pan, heat butter and vegetable oil over medium heat. Turn breasts over to sear the other side.

In a jelly-roll pan, place chicken pieces in a single layer. Bake in a preheated 400° oven for 10 to 15 minutes, depending on thickness of breasts, or until chicken is tender.

To make sauce: In a saucepan over medium heat, melt butter. Add chopped shallots and garlic and sauté for 3 minutes, being careful not to let the shallots brown. Stir in Dijon mustard; add white wine and deglaze pan. Add cream and a pinch of salt and pepper. Reduce sauce by ⅔. Correct seasoning to taste.

Place chicken pieces on a large platter. Pour sauce over chicken and serve immediately.

Serves 4

AL WAXMAN

S HARON Wyatt has come into your homes as Tiffany Mills on *General Hospital*. Originally from Crossville, Tennessee, she is truly the Southern belle and made two Southern specialties when she visited *Hour*'s kitchen—Hoppin' John and Chess Pie.

Hoppin' John

2 cups blackeyed peas
1 onion, diced
4 cups water
1 teaspoon oregano
1 pound spicy country sausage
½ cup rice
  Ground pepper
1 jalapeño pepper, chopped (optional)

Rinse peas and place in a crock pot. Add onion, water, and oregano. Cook overnight.

The next day: Sauté sausage until browned. Add to crock pot (include cooking grease) with the rice, ground pepper, and jalapeño pepper, if desired. Cook for an additional 4 hours. Serve with cornbread.

Serves 6

SHARON WYATT

Chess Pie

¼ pound (1 stick) butter
1 cup sugar
3 eggs
1 tablespoon cider vinegar
1 tablespoon vanilla extract
One 9-inch unbaked pie shell

Preheat oven to 350°.

Cream the butter and sugar together. Add eggs, vinegar, and vanilla. Combine well. Pour into unbaked pie shell. Bake at 350° for 40 to 45 minutes.

Serves 6 to 8

SHARON WYATT

3

RECIPE CONTEST WINNERS

If you have the first *Hour Magazine* cookbook, then you know that in 1984 we conducted our first recipe contest and included the winning recipes in that cookbook. Since the contest was such a success, we announced another in 1987 and were flooded with over 60,000 recipes.

We assembled a panel of judges including Bert Greene, CBS Radio food critic Melinda Lee, Chef Tell, Laurie Burrows Grad, and Wolfgang Puck.

On May 11, 1987, our team of judges came on the show to make the final selections and chose Suzann Gross from Fairlawn, New Jersey, as the grand prize winner. Suzann drove off in a brand-new car and the runners-up each received a microwave oven.

It was fun to see just how many great cooks we have in America; the recipes that follow have been tested by the experts themselves. Why not try them?

Golden Bread Pudding

    One 1-pound challah (Jewish egg bread)
       3 cups 2% low-fat milk
       1 cup heavy cream
   1½ cups sugar
       3 eggs
       2 tablespoons almond extract
     ¾ cup sliced almonds
     ¾ cup golden raisins
     ¾ cup chopped dried apricots

Amaretto Sauce

       1 cup powdered sugar
     ½ cup sweet butter
       1 egg, beaten
     ¼ cup amaretto liqueur

Tear bread into 1-inch pieces. Combine with milk and cream in a large bowl. Let stand while assembling other ingredients. Mix together sugar, eggs, and almond extract thoroughly. Add to bread mixture, making sure all the bread has been coated. Add the almonds, raisins, and chopped apricots. Prepare a 9 × 13 × 2-inch baking dish with spray such as Pam. Preheat oven to 325°. Spoon mixture into dish and bake until firm, about 50 minutes.

Cut into individual servings and spoon amaretto sauce over each portion.

To make sauce: Stir sugar and butter in top of a double boiler until butter melts and sugar dissolves. Remove from water. Whisk in egg, cool slightly, then mix in amaretto.

Serves 8 to 10

Suzann Gross
Fairlawn, New Jersey

Spaghetti with Prosciutto and Porcini alla Salerno

       1 ounce dried porcini mushrooms
       3 tablespoons butter
     ¼ cup olive oil
       3 garlic cloves, minced
     ¼ pound prosciutto cut in thin strips

½ pound fresh mushrooms, quartered
½ teaspoon rosemary
One 10-ounce package frozen peas
1 tablespoon vinegar
⅛ teaspoon black pepper
10 black olives, cut very small
12 ounces spaghetti

Place porcini in small bowl; pour in 1 cup boiling water and let stand for 20 minutes. Strain and reserve liquid. Cut porcini mushrooms in thin strips.

In large skillet, melt butter with olive oil over medium heat. Add garlic and sauté 30 seconds. Stir in prosciutto strips, fresh mushrooms, and rosemary. Cover and cook for 3 minutes. Increase heat to high and sauté uncovered for 2 minutes, or until liquid evaporates. Stir in porcini, peas, and vinegar and sauté for 1 minute. Season with black pepper and sprinkle with olive pieces.

Cook pasta according to package directions. Transfer to warm serving bowl. Add reserved porcini liquid and remaining ingredients and toss well with spaghetti; serve hot.

Serves 6

ROSEMARIE CIPRIANO

Italian Cheese Farina Pie

¼ cup plain breadcrumbs
3 cups low-fat milk
½ cup uncooked farina
6 ounces butter
Pinch salt
¾ cup sugar
4 large eggs, lightly beaten
1½ cups ricotta cheese
1 teaspoon vanilla
1 teaspoon freshly grated lemon rind
1 teaspoon freshly grated orange rind
Pinch cinnamon

Preheat oven to 350°. Grease a 10-inch deep-rimmed pie dish and sprinkle the breadcrumbs evenly over the bottom and sides of the dish.

Heat milk to a boil, lower heat, and gradually pour the farina into the milk.

Stir until all the milk is absorbed. Quickly add the butter and salt and blend well. Set aside this mixture to cool.

Add the rest of the ingredients, one at a time, to the farina and milk mixture; blend with a whisk.

Pour into the pie dish and bake for 30 minutes until golden brown. Chill and serve.

Serves 8 to 10

Mrs. Anna Galgano
Port Rickey, Florida

Shrimp 'n' Grapefruit Madras

⅓ cup butter
½ cup finely chopped onions
6 tablespoons flour
1 tablespoon curry powder
½ teaspoon salt
1 cube chicken bouillon
2½ cups milk
½ cup grapefruit juice
2 pounds cooked shrimp
2 cups grapefruit sections
4 cups cooked rice
¼ cup finely chopped parsley
Chopped peanuts

Melt butter in saucepan; add onions and cook until transparent. Blend in flour, curry, and salt. Add bouillon cube. Heat milk and grapefruit juice together and gradually stir into the onion mixture. Cook over low heat, stirring constantly until thickened. Gently stir in shrimp and grapefruit sections, reserving some fruit for condiments. Cook slowly to heat through. Serve immediately with rice which has been combined with parsley. Serve chopped peanuts as another condiment with this dish.

Serves 4 to 6

Sue Siegel
Maywood, New Jersey

Tex-Mex Lasagne

Sauce

(For best results, make this sauce 1 day before serving.)

- 2 tablespoons virgin olive oil
- 3 large garlic cloves, smashed
- 6 medium-sized white onions, diced
- 1 whole green bell pepper, diced
- 2½ pounds ground extra-lean chuck
   Salt and pepper
- 56 ounces tomatoes (Italian-style peeled, NOT STEWED, tomatoes)
- 30 ounces tomato sauce
- 24 ounces tomato paste
- 2 tablespoons anise seed
- 2 teaspoons celery seed
- 2 teaspoons sesame seed
- 2 tablespoons dry mustard
- 2 teaspoons oregano
- 2 teaspoons cumin
- 1 tablespoon dried cilantro
- ½ tablespoon chili powder
- 1 tablespoon parsley flakes
- 2 tablespoon sugar

Heat the oil over medium heat in a 6-quart pot. Add the garlic and stir in the onions and bell pepper. Cook approximately 10 to 15 minutes. Add the meat, slowly, until all is browned. Add salt and pepper to taste.

Add the tomatoes cut into bite-sized pieces, tomato sauce, and tomato paste; let simmer. Add the spices and sugar and let simmer again for 2 to 3 hours. Let the sauce cool and sit overnight.

Cheese Layers

(This can also be done the day before.)

- 5 to 6 ounces Romano cheese (in bulk, not grated)
- 5 to 6 ounces Parmesan cheese (in bulk, not grated)
- 8 ounces Philadephia Cream Cheese
- 40 ounces small-curd cottage cheese (with chives, optional)

20 ounces extra-sharp cheddar cheese
12 ounces mozzarella cheese

Grate the "hard" cheeses. Cut the cream cheese into ½-inch squares for easier mixing. Combine all the cheeses in a large bowl. (Note: If you mix ¼ of the cheeses at a time, it is easier to manage, i.e., you'll make 4 equal blends.) Taking ¼ of this cheese mixture, pat it out flat on a large sheet of waxed paper. Top with another sheet of waxed paper and, using a rolling pin, roll mixture into a square about 9×13 inches. Remove the top sheet of waxed paper and place layer on a cookie sheet. Repeat the operation until you have 4 layers, separated by 1 sheet of waxed paper, on cookie sheet. Refrigerate.

Noodles

2 tablespoons olive oil
1½ tablespoons salt
32 lasagna noodles

Bring water to a boil, add olive oil and salt, then the lasagna noodles, one at a time. Cook for about 12 to 15 minutes, until noodles are firm, not mushy.

Drain, rinse with cold water, and place back in pot with enough hot salted water to cover the noodles.

To assemble the lasagna: Reheat sauce. Add chopped olives and sliced mushrooms, if desired.

Put a double layer of lasagna noodles in a 9×13×2-inch pan. (Absorb extra moisture out of noodles with a clean tea towel.) Next, smooth 3 ½ cups sauce over the noodles. Grab a layer of cheese and lay it on sauce, waxed paper side up. Remove the waxed paper. Repeat the process for a second layer. (This makes 2 pans of lasagna, and it freezes easily.)

If desired, garnish with a dozen pitted ripe olives pressed into the top cheese layer.

Bake at 325° for 40 to 45 minutes, or until the cheese starts to melt together and browns slightly. Cool slightly before serving.

Serves 14 to 16

WILLIAM F. SPAIN
HOUSTON, TEXAS

4

YOUNG GOURMETS

How many of you encourage your children to cook? Some say that supervised exploration in the kitchen at an early age will begin the makings of a future gourmet!

I know that Mary Ann and I always got a kick out of watching our daughter Clancy concoct a special breakfast or dessert for us. And so I especially enjoyed sharing *Hour*'s kitchen with those I like to call "young gourmets." The recipes that follow may seem a bit juvenile for you to make, but they might provide a perfect excuse for you to be waited on one day by *your* "young gourmets!"

YOU love **Tempestt Bledsoe** each week as Vanessa Huxtable, one of the children on *The Cosby Show*. When she visited *Hour Magazine,* she was representing the California Raisin Advisory Board as well as the President's Council on Physical Fitness. So now you understand why she brought a recipe with a rather unusual combination of ingredients—Raisin Tostadas. But take my word, they're great!

Raisin Tostadas

1 cup chopped onion
One 4-ounce can diced green chilies
2 cloves garlic, pressed
1 tablespoon vegetable oil
1 pound ground beef
One 8-ounce can tomato sauce
⅓ cup raisins
¼ cup sliced pitted ripe olives
Salt to taste
8 slices whole wheat bread, lightly toasted
1½ cups (6 ounces) shredded cheddar cheese

In a large skillet, sauté onions, chilies, and garlic in oil 5 minutes. Add and break up beef. Cook and stir until beef loses pink color, about 5 minutes; drain fat. Stir in tomato sauce, raisins, and olives. Simmer 5 minutes. Stir in salt. Place 4 slices toast on baking sheet. Cover each with ⅓ cup hot beef mixture and another slice of toast. Top with remaining beef mixture and the cheese, dividing equally. Bake in 500° oven 5 to 8 minutes, until cheese is bubbly.

Serves 4

TEMPESTT BLEDSOE

French Toast and Scrambled Eggs

½ teaspoon butter
6 eggs
½ cup milk
½ teaspoon cinnamon
6 slices French bread (sliced ¾" thick)

Over medium heat, melt butter in frying pan. Whip together eggs, milk and cinnamon. Soak, one at a time, the pieces of bread in the egg mixture, until the bread is fairly soggy but not so soft that it falls apart when you pick it up. Cook the soaked pieces of bread in the frying pan until brown on both sides. Serve, sprinkled with powdered sugar and your favorite syrup.

With the remaining egg mixture, make scrambled eggs:

Heat egg mixture in the greased frying pan over medium heat until eggs are of desired consistency. (Don't overstir eggs.)

Serves 3

BRIAN BONSALL

Chicken à la Tiffany

2 whole boneless chicken breasts, split and pounded
1 cup flour (seasoned with salt and pepper)

¼ cup olive oil
4 thin slices Danish-style ham
4 round slices pineapple
4 slices Monterey jack cheese

Pound breasts thin. Dredge in seasoned flour. Sauté in oil (3 minutes per side). Top each slice with ham, pineapple, then cheese. Broil until cheese is golden brown and bubbly.

Serves 2 to 4

TIFFANY BRISSETTE

WHEN they visited *Hour Magazine* **Ricky Caffey** was only seven and **Amanda Hammerman** was ten. They had just completed an international cooking class at Yorba Linda Schools Children's Center in Yorba Linda, California. They told me that they learned how to cook everything from tofu to tortillas, and I felt sure they did once they started showing me what to do to make Silver Paper Chicken, a recipe you can be proud of!

     ## Silver Paper Chicken

2 pounds deboned chicken
3 tablespoons hoisin sauce
½ teaspoon five-spice powder
¼ cup sesame oil
3 tablespoons peanut oil plus extra for deep-frying
1 clove garlic
6 leaves cilantro
2 tablespoons flour

Cut chicken into bite-sized pieces.
Combine remaining ingredients and marinate chicken 2 hours.
Wrap chicken into 4×4-inch foil squares.
Deep-fry for 7 minutes in 375° peanut oil.

Serves 4 to 6.

RICKY CAFFEY AND AMANDA HAMMERMAN

DINERS are back across America (some say they never left!) and one of the newest additions to the L.A. scene is a diner called ED DEBEVIC'S. Kids are the biggest draw to this diner, and I have to admit that I get a bit nostalgic myself from time to time for the days of hamburgers and chocolate shakes.

Many of the waiters and waitresses at ED DEBEVIC'S are aspiring performers who often get up on tables to entertain while you're eating. So we welcomed **Irving** and **Madeline**, who worked at the diner, and asked them to reveal recipes for some of their specialty items.

Diner Delites

Bleu Cheese Dressing for Burgers

1 quart plus 1 cup mayonnaise
8 ounces crumbled blue cheese
Pinch salt
Pinch white pepper
¾ cup half-and-half

♥ ♥ Atomic Sauce for French Fries

3 ounces minced jalapeños
8 ounces minced onions
3 ounces minced tomatoes
½ bunch cilantro

Combine and pour on melted cheddar or processed cheese.

♥ ♥ Ed's Burger Sauce for Bun

1 cup dry mustard
1 cup hot water
½ cup salad oil
¾ cup white vinegar
1¼ cups sugar
1 teaspoon salt

♥ ♥ Marlborough Onions

  8 ounces flour
  1 teaspoon salt
  1 teaspoon fine black pepper
  Sliced onions
  Vegetable oil

Mix flour with salt and pepper. Dip onions in flour, then throw into heated vegetable oil.

Chocolate Malt

  9 ounces Häagen-Dazs Chocolate Ice Cream
  6 ounces milk
  1 ounce Hershey's Chocolate Syrup
  2 ounces Horlick's malt
  1 ounce whipped cream

Combine first 4 ingredients in mixer. Top with whipped cream.

Serves 1

IRVING AND MADELINE FROM ED DEBEVIC'S DINER

Reprinted by permission of Ed Debevic's Short Orders Deluxe.

B RENNAN Loring is the son of Gloria Loring, whom you know from *Days of Our Lives,* and Alan Thicke from *Growing Pains.* When Brennan was only four, it was discovered he had diabetes. Today, almost fourteen years old, he has daily injections of insulin, tests his blood a few times a day, and keeps a close watch on his diet. He loves to help his mom in the kitchen and when she was my co-host, he came on to make Sweet Potato Pie. Gloria and Brennan continue to stay active in the Juvenile Diabetes Foundation to help others who have to face the same chronic illness cope more easily.

Sweet Potato Pie

  1 egg white
  2 whole eggs

3 medium sweet potatoes or yams, cooked and peeled
6 packets artificial sweetner (equal to ¼ cup sugar)
One 8-ounce can crushed pineapple in juice, drained
¾ cup evaporated skim milk
1 teaspoon vanilla extract
¼ teaspoon each ground nutmeg, ginger, and cinnamon
1 unbaked pie shell

Preheat oven to 425°. Beat egg white and eggs in food processor. Mash sweet potatoes and add to egg mixture. Add remaining ingredients except pie shell and mix well to combine. Pour into pie shell and bake for 10 minutes. Reduce heat to 325° and bake another 45 minutes. A knife inserted in the center should come out relatively clean.

Serves 8

BRENNAN LORING

DANNY Pintauro from *Who's the Boss?* was only ten when he visited the *Hour Magazine* kitchen. And so you can understand why his Jell-O Surprise and Melon Roll-ups are so simplistic. He's been a show business veteran since the age of two when he co-starred on the daytime soap *As the World Turns.* But he loves to cook and learned all his techniques from his beloved grandfather.

♥ ♥   **Danny's Jell-O Surprise**

1 package sugarless orange Jell-O
Ice
1 banana, sliced

Follow Jell-O package instructions for quick method using ice.
Whip in blender. Pour into dessert or parfait glasses.
Add sliced banana.
Refrigerate for ½ hour.

Serves 4 to 6

DANNY PINTAURO

♥ # Melon Roll-ups

1 honeydew or cantaloupe melon
8 slices prosciutto or smoked ham, sliced thin
1 lemon, cut in eighths
   Sliced onions for garnish

Slice melon into 8 pieces. Remove rind. Wrap with ham.
Squeeze lemon over and garnish with onions.

Serves 8

DANNY PINTAURO

TANNIS Vallely plays Janice Lazorott, the half-pint whiz kid from
Head of the Class. She had the distinct honor of being the top-
selling girl scout in her troop for two consecutive years. So, naturally
she brought along recipes for desserts that included girl scout cookies.
And wouldn't you know it, once we finished cooking, she tried to sell
me some cookies. (Yes, I *did* buy some!)

Chunky Munky Pudding Pie

Line a 9-inch pie tin with girl scout shortbread cookies. Prepare regular-size
instant banana pudding/pie filling mix according to instructions on box. Slice
several bananas. Over the shortbread layer, add a layer of bananas, a layer of
pudding, and then top with more bananas and cookies.

Serves 6 to 8

TANNIS VALLELY

Junior Peanut Ice

2 cups vanilla ice cream
1 cup girl scout chunky peanut butter sandwich cookies,
   crumbled

Mix together. Freeze again. Dish out a big scoop of ice cream. Top with warm
creamy chocolate sauce.

Serves 2

TANNIS VALLELY

5

HOUR FAMILY IN THE KITCHEN

What would an *Hour Magazine* cookbook be without some recipes from the people responsible for putting together the daily show?

When I travel around the country I'm always amazed at the amount of questions people ask me about the staff. And they often wonder what it takes to put a show like ours together. Besides hard work and dedication, it takes a staff of people who have a desire to entertain others, to inform others, and to keep on learning themselves in order to present the most up-to-date material to our audience. And when I think of this staff, I think of a great group of people who, above all, *care* about others.

Here are some recipes from those responsible for making every *Hour* count. As you'll see, many are true chefs themselves (although I can't imagine how they do it and work the hours they do). And some have chosen a favorite recipe from their family to share with our audience.

H ERE'S one of my favorite recipes that's great for entertaining. The pesto sauce makes the fish taste unusual, and if you can't get orange roughy you can substitute another fish.

♥ ♥ ## Steamed Orange Roughy with Pesto Sauce

1 quart water
½ cup white wine or fish stock
1 small slice onion
2 cloves garlic
2 slices lemon peel
8 orange roughy fillets
1 tablespoon chopped chives for garnish
Pesto Sauce (recipe follows)

Fill bottom of steamer with water, wine, onion, garlic, and lemon peel. Bring to a boil. Place fish in the steamer rack. Cover tightly and steam 8 to 10 minutes. Remove to platter. Garnish with chopped chives, serve with Pesto Sauce.

♥ ## Pesto Sauce

3–4 cloves garlic
2 cups fresh basil leaves
½ cup parsley sprigs
½ cup toasted pine nuts (or walnuts)
2 tablespoons grated Parmesan or Romano cheese
Salt and pepper to taste
½ cup extra-virgin olive oil

Place garlic in the bowl of a food processor fitted with the steel blade. Mince garlic; scrape the sides of the bowl. Add remaining ingredients, except for the oil. Process to a fine mince. Scrape the sides of the bowl once again. Add oil gradually through the feed tube while processing until smooth.

Serves 8

GARY COLLINS

MORRIS Abraham is our talented director. He is so committed to the show that it's difficult to keep him away from the offices even on a week when we're *not* in production. His ancestry is Middle Eastern, and this is one of his family's recipes for an appetizer that would be great at a traditional dinner. Morris says it's a must to serve it with pita bread!

 ## Hummus Bi Tahina

2 cloves garlic
4 cups cooked or two 16-ounce cans chickpeas (garbanzo
   beans), liquid reserved
1 teaspoon hot paprika
4 tablespoons virgin olive oil
¼ cup freshly squeezed lemon juice
¾ cup tahini paste
   Salt and white pepper to taste
2 tablespoons chopped parsley

Place garlic in food processor; mince finely. Add drained chick peas and process 1 minute; scrape sides of processor. Add paprika, 2 tablespoons olive oil, lemon juice, and tahini; continue processing. Add reserved juice through feed tube while processing until mixture is the consistency of pancake batter. Add salt and pepper. Pour onto serving plate. Drizzle with remaining olive oil. Top with parsley and a sprinkle of paprika. Serve as an appetizer with pita bread.

Makes about 2 to 3 cups

MORRIS ABRAHAM

YVONNE Alvarez is an assistant to the executive producer and often to me as well (e.g., researching for this cookbook, typing the manuscript, etc.). She's one of the sweetest members on the staff who seems to get everything done—no matter what the pressures are like—with a smile. Even though she's still raising two daughters (Danielle twelve, Colleen, eight), she tells me she doesn't like to spend all day in the kitchen, so this Ambrosia fits the bill. Every time she's asked to bring something to a party, she chooses this recipe because you can whip it up quickly and, she adds, everybody always loves it!

Ambrosia

1 large can fruit cocktail, drained
1 small can crushed pineapple, drained
1 small can mandarin oranges, drained
½ pint (8 ounces) sour cream
  Miniature marshmallows
  Shredded coconut
  Chopped walnuts (optional)

Combine all drained fruit and sour cream; mix well. Add about half the bag of marshmallows. Add desired amount of coconut and also desired amount of walnuts, if using. Keep refrigerated until ready to serve.

Serves 10

YVONNE C. ALVAREZ

LINDA Bell is one of our producers who dared to share a recipe for this luscious chocolate cake. Linda's new to *Hour,* and a welcome addition because of her pleasant nature and willingness to please. She tells me this cake is a crowd pleaser too—and I don't doubt it for a minute!

Linda Bell's Chocolate Cake

The secret ingredient is the sour cream.

Cake

2 cups flour
2 cups sugar
1¼ teaspoons baking soda
1 teaspoon salt
½ teaspoon baking powder
1 cup water
¾ cup dairy sour cream
¼ cup shortening
1 teaspoon vanilla extract
2 eggs
4 ounces unsweetened chocolate, melted and cooled

Heat oven to 350°. Grease and flour two 8- or 9-inch round cake pans and line the bottom with waxed paper. Sift flour into measuring cups; level off. In a medium bowl combine flour, sugar, baking soda, salt, and baking powder; blend well. Set aside. In a large bowl, combine remaining cake ingredients; add dry ingredients. Blend with a mixer at low speed until moistened; beat 3 minutes at highest speed. Pour batter into prepared pans. Bake for 30 to 40 minutes, or until toothpick inserted in the middle comes out clean. Cool 10 minutes; remove from pans. Cool completely.

Frosting

3 cups confectioners' sugar
¼ cup dairy sour cream
¼ cup butter or margarine, softened
3 tablespoons milk
1 teaspoon vanilla extract
3 ounces unsweetened chocolate, melted and cooled

In a small bowl, combine all frosting ingredients and beat at low speed of mixer until moistened: Beat at highest speed until smooth and creamy. Place 1 cake layer top side down on serving plate; spread evenly with about ¼ of frosting. Top with remaining cake layer top side up. Spread sides and top of cake with remaining frosting.

Serves 12

LINDA BELL

MARTY Berman, our Emmy award–winning executive producer, who was part of the team that created the show says that his wife Elyse has become very creative making meals that correlate with his erratic hours. Besides having a great professional relationship, Marty and I love to play golf together (a new passion for Marty); it's good to get away from the rigorous show schedule and unwind.

Elyse says this is the perfect dish that you can cook slowly and won't burn no matter how late the family eats. As I would expect from Marty, his recipe received a heart healthy rating.

♥ ♥ ## Elyse's Chicken in the Bag

    1 whole 4–5-pound chicken (remove skin)
    1 tablespoon flour
    1 oven cooking bag (this can be purchased in any
      supermarket)
    ½ pound string beans
    ½ pound carrots
 6–10 small potatoes

Season the chicken with seasonings of your choice (garlic, pepper, paprika, etc.). Throw in 1 tablespoon flour to prevent the bag from popping. Put the chicken in the bag and place all the vegetables around the chicken. Close the bag with a twist tie. Make 5 or 6 slits in the bag.

You can make this dish without using any oil or frying anything. It is a one-pan (that is very easy to clean) dish, which cooks in its own juices. It can also be ready to cook the night before.

Bake at 350° for 1½ hours.

Serves 6

MARTY BERMAN

Caramel Walnut Torte

Torte

1 cup flour
⅔ cup ground almonds
⅓ cup sugar
½ teaspoon baking powder
½ cup butter, chilled
1 egg yolk
2–3 tablespoons cold water

Combine first 4 ingredients. Cut in butter until mixture is coarse in appearance. In small bowl beat egg yolk and 2 tablespoons water. Spread over flour mixture. Toss until it binds. Shape dough into ball, cover, and refrigerate 30 minutes. Spread ⅔ of the dough into a 10-inch circle and place in ungreased 10-inch springform pan. Roll out remaining ⅓ of dough and form to the sides of pan. Pierce shell with fork. Bake at 375° 12 minutes, or until lightly browned.

Filling

1 ounce semisweet chocolate, melted
1 pound granulated sugar
¾ cup whipping cream
6 ounces unsalted butter
1 pound chopped walnuts

Pour melted chocolate over torte shell.
Caramelize sugar. Carefully add cream and butter with wooden spoon and stir until blended. Fold in chopped walnuts. Pour into prepared torte shell.
Serve with freshly whipped cream.

Serves 8

ALLISON BIRNIE

Frikadeller (Danish Meatballs)

1½ pounds ground round
½ pound ground pork
1 grated onion
4 tablespoons flour
⅛ teaspoon pepper
1½ teaspoon salt
2 eggs
Milk
Oil or margarine

Mix onion and ground meats together. Blend in next 4 ingredients. Beat in milk a little at a time until a fluffy consistency for shaping meatballs. Heat oil or margarine in a frying pan. Use wooden spoon to shape meat into small oval balls. Fry until light brown on both sides.

Serve with red cabbage, parsley-buttered potatoes, and gravy if desired.

Serves 4

JAN BISGAARD

Broccoli Spoon Bread

    1 bunch broccoli (about ½ pound)
1½ cups milk
    ½ cup yellow cornmeal
    2 eggs, separated
    2 teaspoons baking powder
    1 teaspoon salt
    1 tablespoon sugar
    Parmesan Sauce (recipe follows)

Trim broccoli, cutting stems 2 inches long. Slit stems almost to florets if stalks are thick. Place broccoli in large saucepan with a small amount of boiling salted water. Cover and cook until crisp-tender, about 5 minutes. Drain, reserving ½ cup liquid for sauce. Gradually stir milk into cornmeal and cook and stir over medium heat until thickened, about 5 minutes. Cool slightly. Beat egg yolks and add to cornmeal with baking powder, salt, and sugar. Mix well. Beat egg whites until stiff but not dry. Fold into cornmeal mixture. Arrange broccoli in a well-greased, deep 2-quart soufflé dish. Spoon batter over, smoothing to edges. Bake at 375° 45 to 50 minutes, until brown. Serve with Parmesan Sauce.

KAREN GRACE CADLE

Parmesan Sauce

    2 tablespoons butter or margarine
    1 tablespoon cornstarch
    1 cup milk
    1 cup grated Parmesan cheese

½ cup broccoli liquid or water
½ teaspoon salt
⅛ teaspoon white pepper
¼ teaspoon nutmeg

Melt butter in small saucepan. Stir in cornstarch to form a smooth paste. Gradually stir in milk. Over low heat cook and stir until sauce is thickened and comes to a boil. Cook, stirring, 3 minutes longer. Add cheese, a little at a time, stirring until melted. Stir in broccoli liquid, salt, pepper, and nutmeg. Heat. Serve warm.

Serves 4 to 6

KAREN GRACE CADLE

CLAUDIA Cagan, a talent coordinator who recently joined the show, says she loves to entertain and is always looking for simple yet elegant meals that can be prepared ahead and cooked once the guests are already at her house, eating hors d'oeuvres. It was given to her by a good friend, and she's passed it along over the years and everyone's been thrilled with the results. And we're sure thrilled to have Claudia aboard!

Claudia's Quickie Chickie

4 chicken breasts cut in half (may use already skinned and
    deboned breasts)
½ pound butter, melted
    Cornflake crumbs (packaged)
    Freshly grated Parmesan cheese
    Parsley sprigs for garnish

Skin and debone breasts, if necessary. Dip in melted butter. Coat with mixture of ½ crumbs and ½ cheese. Brush pieces of aluminum foil big enough to cover chicken with melted butter. Press the ends together. Place packages of chicken on baking sheet and bake in 450° oven for 20 to 25 minutes.

To serve: Remove carefully from foil wrappers and garnish with fresh parsley. I like to serve this dish with saffron rice and some steamed broccoli. ENJOY!!

This recipe serves 8 if you think that your guests will only have 1 breast apiece. I usually figure on 2 apiece and reheat the leftovers!

CLAUDIA CAGAN

CAROLE Chouinard is our coordinating producer who has the ability to make you feel secure; if you ask Carole to find something or do something, you can be sure it will be done well. She's been with us through two pregnancies and two pregnancy leaves and is very proud of her daughter Annelise and baby son Darin.

She gave me her recipe for Golden Glazed Chicken, which just happened to win her mother-in-law, Charlotte T. Baer, the New Hampshire state chicken-cooking contest. A prizewinning, heart-healthy chicken treat!

♥ ♥   **Golden Glazed Chicken**

  2 tablespoons margarine
½ cup honey
¼ cup Dijon mustard
½ teaspoon salt
  1 teaspoon curry powder
  3 half chicken breasts or package of filleted breasts, skinned

Over low heat in a saucepan on the stove melt the margarine, then add the honey and mustard. Stir until mixed. Add the salt and curry powder and stir in. Take off heat. Put the skinned chicken pieces in the baking dish, coating well with the honey mixture. Bake at 350° for 1 hour, periodically basting the chicken with the mixture. Great served with rice.

Serves 2 to 4

CAROLE CHOUINARD

C HRIS (how could I get through any cooking spots without him?) Circosta is the show's extraordinary prop master. Chris has got to open his own restaurant someday; he loves to cook and what he likes about this recipe is the fact that it incorporates different textures—and the cognac gives it an unusual flavor.

He says that for an elegant presentation of this meal, you should use a copper pot with a copper skillet. Chris is truly a perfectionist, and we are very grateful he's a part of *Hour* family.

Fettuccine with Four Mushrooms in Cognac Cream

    2 tablespoons extra-virgin olive oil
    2 tablespoons unsalted butter
    ¼ cup minced shallots
    1 clove garlic, minced
    3 ounces dried porcini mushrooms (reconstituted by placing
        mushrooms in a bowl, adding boiling water, and soaking
        for 15 minutes), drained and sliced
    3 ounces chanterelle mushrooms, sliced
    3 ounces shiitake mushrooms, sliced
    3 ounces domestic white mushrooms, minced
    1 ounce cognac
    ¾ cup heavy cream
    1 tablespoon chopped fresh basil or 1 teaspoon dried
    1 tablespoon chopped fresh oregano or 1 teaspoon dried
    1 tablespoon chopped fresh parsley
        Salt and freshly ground pepper
    ½ pound (8 ounces) cooked black squid ink or tomato
        fettuccine

Heat oil and butter together in a large heavy sauté pan. Sauté shallots and garlic over medium heat for 2 minutes. Add all of the mushrooms. Sauté 3 to 4 minutes. Add cognac. Carefully ignite pan to burn off alcohol. Cook for 1 minute. Add cream. Cook over medium heat until sauce begins to thicken; add basil, oregano, and parsley, and salt and pepper. Simmer for 2 minutes. Serve over hot pasta.

Serves 4

CHRIS CIRCOSTA

C HRIS DeMore is a talented musician who sings around town at local clubs when she's not working at *Hour* as our production administrator. She was born Christine Somma of Italian and German ancestry, and when she was growing up in Pittsburgh, her father ate a lot of pizza and liked his very plain. So her mother made Pizza Bianco for them a lot.

In the present DeMore household, Chris and her husband, Dave, who is also a musician, writer, and recording engineer, created their own version of this family recipe. Her tips: Use very sharp imported provolone and try it as an appetizer or for a main course with salad.

Pizza Bianca

Dough

1 package dry yeast
¾ cup warm water
¼ teaspoon sugar
1 tablespoon olive oil
1 teaspoon salt
3 cups flour

Topping

2 medium-sized white onions
2 tablespoons olive oil
4 large garlic cloves, pressed
½ teaspoon freshly ground pepper
1 teaspoon dried basil
6–8 fresh basil leaves
10–12 sprigs Italian parsley
6–8 sprigs fresh oregano
1 red bell pepper
1 cup grated imported very sharp provolone cheese

Make dough: Sprinkle yeast over warm water and let stand for a minute. Stir in sugar and olive oil. Combine salt and flour and in a mixing bowl combine liquid and 1½ cups of flour. Place on lightly floured surface and knead in remainder of flour until dough is elastic and does not feel sticky to the touch. Lightly oil a bowl and place dough inside. Let rise for 40 minutes in a warm place.

Preheat oven to 450°.

Make topping: Chop onions and place in a saucepan with olive oil and garlic. Sauté on low heat, adding pepper and dried basil. Keep covered to retain moisture. When onions are clear, remove from heat and let stand a few minutes. Place cooled contents into food processor and pulverize. Put in a bowl and set aside. This is your "sauce" for the pizza. You will notice that the onions, garlic, and basil have become a very sweet paste.

Chop basil leaves, parsley, and oregano and set aside. Slice red pepper thinly and set aside.

When dough has risen, punch down and flatten, gently forming into a large round pizza. Place in lightly greased pizza pan, or if you have a pizza clay preheating in the oven, place pizza on a pizza paddle, slightly covered with cornmeal so it will move gently from the paddle to the lightly cornmeal-covered pizza clay in the oven.

Spread onion mixture over the top of the pizza, leaving 1 inch for a crust. Sprinkle basil, parsley, and oregano on top. Arrange red bell peppers on top and sprinkle with cheese.

Bake for 8 to 12 minutes.

Serves 8

CHRIS DeMORE

CAROL DeRiggi is an associate producer whose background is Italian. You can tell because she's always got a great big grin on her face and her love for life is obvious. She tells me her recipe is her mother's dish for Strufoli, which are marble-sized dough balls that are fried until golden and covered with honey and candy confetti. Carol says it's one of three recipes her mom brought to America when she left Italy. Here in America, though, she adapted it for use in a Cuisinart food processor. Strufoli are a traditional dish eaten at Christmastime.

Strufoli

Pinch salt
4 eggs
1 tablespoon sugar
2 ounces softened butter
2½ cups flour
½ teaspoon grated lemon peel (optional)

½ teaspoon grated orange peel (optional)
Vegetable oil
1 cup honey plus 2 tablespoons sugar
Candied fruit
Candy confetti

Dissolve salt in 2 tablespoons warm water. Combine in food processor bowl eggs, sugar, softened butter, flour, and grated lemon and/or orange peel, if using. Mix into a smooth dough. (Add more flour if needed until consistency of dough resembles a soft bread dough.) Cover and let dough stand 1 hour.

Flour rolling surface. Break off a small portion of dough. Roll dough out into rounded strips, similar in shape to breadsticks. Then cut dough into pieces ¼ inch long.

Heat about 2 inches oil in a deep pan or vegetable fryer. Add the pieces of dough, a batch at a time, and fry until golden. Place pieces on a paper towel to drain.

Heat honey and sugar plus 2 tablespoons water in a pan. Bring to a boil (until foam disappears). Lower heat. Add Strufoli and as much candied fruit as desired. Mix with honey coating, stirring quickly, until most of the honey is absorbed. Transfer mixture immediately to a plate. Wet hands with cold water and shape into a mound. Sprinkle with candy confetti.

Makes 40 pieces

CAROL DeRIGGI

PROMOTION writer **Maureen Poon-Fear**, and her mom, Mary Poon, are not great cooks but they love to eat. In fact, Mary Poon even grows cherry tomatoes in her backyard, but instead of cooking with them, she gives them to Maureen to bring into the staff, who never have to buy tomatoes all spring, thanks to Mary!

Their friend Reiko, born in America and raised in Japan, gave her this sukiyaki recipe which is easy to make. And Maureen says that the taste is pretty unusual.

Reiko's Sukiyaki

2 tablespoons sugar
1 tablespoon soy sauce
Water or wine

1–2 tablespoons fat (lard, butter, margarine)
One 2-pound rib eye, thinly sliced (sukiyaki meat)
 1 package hard tofu, drained and cut into squares
 1 package shiitake mushrooms, soaked in water and
  chopped
 1 package ito konnyaku, drained and chopped
 1 Spanish onion, chopped
 1 bunch green onions, chopped
 1 bunch spinach, chopped

Combine sugar, soy sauce, and water or wine to taste. Set aside. Melt cube of fat in hot skillet. Add the rib eye. When meat is almost cooked, add soy sauce, sugar, and water or wine mixture. Add tofu, shiitake, and konnyaku. Then add Spanish onion, green onions, and spinach.

Cook until vegetables are done, adding more of the sugar, soy sauce, and water or wine mixture as needed.

Serves 4

MAUREEN POON-FEAR

SENIOR producer **Larry Ferber** claims he's a great cook (should we check with his wife, Marcia?). Well if he's as quick and effective in the kitchen as he is in *Hour*'s studio, then I'd believe him! It's always great to be around Larry when he laughs; he's got one of those uncontrollable bellows that gives you a sense that he really knows what matters in life! Larry told me that after eating a veal dish at one of Los Angeles's trendy eateries, he went home and said, "I'll bet I can make this even better." And so you have it, Veal à la Larry.

♥   **Veal à la Larry**

 ¼ cup flour
  Pinch black pepper
 1 pound veal, thinly sliced
 1 tablespoon oil
 1 tablespoon butter
 1 clove garlic, minced
 1 cup canned, peeled tomatoes, drained and cut up

½ cup black olives
½ cup artichoke hearts, cut up
½ cup chopped red pepper (optional)
¼ cup red wine

Combine flour and pepper in a plastic bag. Put in veal 1 piece at a time to coat lightly.

In a large skillet combine oil and butter on medium-high heat (make sure butter doesn't burn by mixing carefully). Add minced garlic and cook for about 30 seconds, or until it starts to turn brown. Add veal and brown quickly, about 30 seconds on each side. Remove veal; reduce heat.

Add tomatoes, olives, artichokes, red peppers, if using, and red wine. Simmer, covered, for about 5 minutes. Return veal to mixture, cover with vegetables, and simmer, covered, about 10 minutes.

Serve with pasta and broccoli.

Serves 2 to 4

LARRY FERBER

KEVIN Fortson, our production manager, lives up to his job. Of course he does so by being stringent with monies and always encouraging the producers and director to cut corners or do without. I was surprised to see that he cooked; I thought he spent most of his time buried in the budget books trying to make ends meet! But all kidding aside, he is super at his job.

His recipe *does* seem to reflect him, though—read on.

Chili Colorado Burritos

4 tablespoons vegetable oil
1 pound round steak or chuck roast (or any inexpensive beef roast cut), trimmed of excess fat, cut into 1" cubes
1 medium onion, chopped finely (careful not to grind it down to a pulp)
1 clove garlic, minced (probably you can borrow this from a neighbor)
¼ cup chopped mild green chilies

One 8-ounce can tomato sauce (get plain wrap sauce; sauce is sauce)

3 heaping tablespoons chili powder (don't cut corners here; this is the soul of the dish)

¼ teaspoon hot pepper flakes

Salt to taste

½ can beer (6 ounces) (no fancy imported types)

½ cup beef broth

1 tablespoon flour mixed with 1 tablespoon water

2 large flour tortillas

¼ cup grated cheddar cheese

1 tablespoon chopped green onion

Heat 2 tablespoons oil in a heavy skillet. Brown meat 3 to 4 minutes. Drain and reserve. Heat remaining oil in a medium saucepan. Add onion, garlic, and chilies. Sauté until onions are soft and transparent. Add browned meat, tomato sauce, chili powder, hot pepper flakes, salt, beer, and broth. Simmer, uncovered, 45 minutes to 1 hour. (Add more liquid if necessary.) Stir in flour/water mixture to thicken sauce. Place meat in tortillas and fold into burritos. Place on heatproof dish. Top with additional sauce and cheese. Place under broiler until cheese is melted and bubbly, 30 seconds. Top with green onions.

Makes 2 burritos (or 4 if you cut them in half). Enjoy with the remaining ½ can of beer.

KEVIN FORTSON

JENNIFER Kemp, our script supervisor, recently graduated from the University of Southern California. I love Jennifer's energy and style, and she's been a breath of fresh air this past season. She brought a recipe from her mom, Arlene Marquez Kemp, whose Hispanic background makes this dish truly authentic. Jennifer says this delicious recipe for chalupas is simple to make and is sure to have every guest or family member raving!

Arlene's Chicken Chalupas

1 can cream of chicken soup

1 can cream of celery soup

One 7-ounce can diced Ortega green chilies
1 pint sour cream
  Green onion tops, diced
1 can sliced olives
1 small onion, grated
¾ pound jack cheese, grated
¾ pound cheddar cheese, grated
3 cups cooked and shredded chicken breast meat
12 flour tortillas
  Paprika
2 teaspoons grated cumin (optional)

Combine soups, chilies, sour cream, onion tops, olives, and grated onion with half of the cheeses. Set aside 1½ cups of this mixture; add chicken to the rest. Place 3 heaping tablespoons of mixture over tortillas and roll. Place in shallow greased 9 × 13-inch baking dish. Pour remaining sauce over top and sprinkle with remaining cheese, green onion tops, paprika, and cumin.

Refrigerate overnight. Bake at 350° for 45 minutes.

Serves 6

JENNIFER KEMP

STEPHANIE Modory, who admits that she doesn't cook, believes her mother Carolyn's recipe for Southwest Cheese Dip is the first thing to be eaten at every party she's brought it to. The best part, claims Stephanie, is the fact that you can take the ingredients with you and actually make it at the party. Stephanie prepared this dip for the office and nobody could continue to work until the dip and chips were gone.

Stephanie, who is our contract coordinator, started with us as an intern while still in college. She was always so conscientious and efficient that from the start we knew we wanted her as part of *Hour*'s family. And we haven't ever been disappointed.

Southwest Cheese Dip

One 8-ounce package cream cheese
Three 8-ounce jars Kraft Old English cheese
One 8-ounce can or jar of mild to medium-strength salsa

1 small can diced green chilies
1 small can diced or minced black olives

Combine all ingredients in a medium saucepan and carefully melt together over low heat, stirring as it blends. After all of the cheese has melted, transfer the mixture to a fondue pot or chafing dish. Serve with tortilla strips or corn chips.

Variations:

Instead of olives, chilies, and salsa, add one 6-ounce can minced clams and 1 or 2 finely sliced green onions.

Serves a whole party

STEPHANIE MODORY

PAUL **Nichols**, our dedicated director of creative services and promotion, spends a lot of time with me on the road, traveling to our different stations. When we're in town he loves to relax on his classic twenty-seven-foot Chris-Craft in Marina del Rey. While on the boat, he does a great deal of barbecuing, so he created a marinade that goes well with any meat or poultry. He's been cooking with it for years and he says it's the hit of the dock parties!

♥ ♥   ## Paul's Marina Marinade
and Barbecue Sauce

¼ cup soy sauce
¼ cup white wine vinegar
¼ cup sherry
¼ cup honey
2 cloves garlic, crushed
⅛ teaspoon ground ginger

Combine ingredients in small saucepan and simmer for about 5 minutes. Marinate meat overnight. Baste meat with sauce frequently while barbecueing over charcoal or mesquite.

Makes about 1 cup

PAUL NICHOLS

ASSOCIATE producer **Kathy O'Reilly** is a dedicated worker who loves to do investigative research for the show. She's so committed to her job that she probably spends more time here than home. Hence, her recipe is for the working woman. And she assumes that every working woman is sure to have a microwave oven. If you have one, why not try Kathy's Micro Chicken Breasts and Cashews? Total cooking time is twenty-eight minutes tops!

Kathy's Micro Chicken Breasts and Cashews

2 tablespoons dry white wine or water
1 tablespoon soy sauce
3 tablespoons oil
1 tablespoon cornstarch
⅛ teaspoon pepper
⅛ teaspoon hot sauce
2 whole boneless chicken breasts, skinned and flattened to ¼ inch thickness
1 medium onion, sliced into rings
1 red or green pepper, sliced into strips
1 cup whole unsalted cashews
½ cup chicken stock or bouillon

In a small bowl, combine wine, soy sauce, 1 tablespoon oil, cornstarch, pepper, and hot sauce. Cut each whole chicken breast into 4 to 6 pieces. Add each piece to wine marinade, then place chicken in a 9 or 10-inch microproof pie plate. Pour remaining marinade over pieces; allow to marinate 15 to 20 minutes. In a 2-quart microproof bowl, combine onion, pepper slices, and 2 tablespoons oil. Use COOK cycle and cook 6 minutes, stirring once. Add cashews and chicken stock. Pour marinade into onion-oil mixture. Stir to blend well. Use COOK cycle and cook chicken pieces for 4 minutes. Turn pieces over and rearrange. Use COOK cycle and cook 2 to 3 minutes, or until chicken loses its pink color. Cover and set aside. Use COOK cycle and cook sauce mixture, covered, for 6 to 7 minutes, or until thickened. Spoon sauce over chicken. Use COOK cycle and cook 2 to 3 minutes, or until heated through. Serve over hot cooked rice.

Serves 4

KATHY O'REILLY

PRODUCER **Cathy Pomponio**, who has been responsible for many of the special series we've done over the years, is also considered our resident feminist. And even though she edited the first cookbook and this one, we weren't shocked to find out that she doesn't enjoy cooking. Growing up in an Italian family, she learned how to enjoy eating but somehow missed the fundamentals of cooking. But she can make this easy Date and Nut Bread, one of her mother Nellie's best recipes. It is great with cream cheese for breakfast or for dessert.

Date and Nut Bread

        1 cup boiling water
One 8-ounce package dates, cut up in small pieces
        1 teaspoon baking soda
        1 cup sugar
One 4-ounce stick of butter, melted
        2 eggs
        2 cups sifted flour
        1 cup chopped walnuts

Pour boiling water over dates, then add baking soda.
Let stand 5 minutes.
Combine remaining ingredients and add date mixture.
Bake in a well-greased tube or loaf pan at 375° for 45 minutes.

Makes 10 slices

CATHY POMPONIO

Mother-in-Law's Slaw

Head of cabbage
1 small can pineapple chunks
1 small jar mayonnaise
Handful of golden raisins
Dash of pepper

Shred whole head of cabbage in a large bowl. Drain pineapple chunks and add. Stir in a desired amount of mayonnaise and add raisins. Sprinkle with a dash of pepper.

Serves 6 to 8

LINDA CALLAHAN SCHWAB

♥ ## Chicken and Rice à la Watte

4–5 chicken legs with thighs attached, skin and fat removed
1–2 tablespoons vegetable oil
1 onion, chopped
One 6-ounce can tomato sauce
1 clove garlic, crushed

Zest from 1 orange
Salt and pepper
2 cups uncooked rice
2 tablespoons parsley

Brown legs and thighs in oil. Add chopped onion and sauté until onion is limp. Drain oil.
Add tomato sauce and enough water to cover chicken.
Add garlic, orange zest, and salt and pepper to taste.
Simmer 1½ to 2 hours until meat can easily be removed from bones.
Skim fat while simmering.
Debone chicken, chop coarsely, and return to pot.
Add rice to chicken mixture and cook until rice is tender.
Add parsley during the last 5 minutes of cooking. Add more orange zest if desired.

Serves 5 to 6

CAROL UCHITA

6

SOUND NUTRITION

Over the years, I've seen a dramatic attitude change about people's concern with their bodies and what they are putting into them. I always remember the time Isadore Rosenfeld remarked that most of us pay more attention to our cars and the kind of fuel we put into them than we do to the "fuel" we put into our bodies. But that's really changing. In *this* chapter we wanted to offer some advice from the experts we rely on here at *Hour Magazine*.

Dr. Isadore Rosenfeld is the bestselling author of The Complete Medical Exam, Second Opinion, *and* Modern Prevention: The New Medicine. *Dr. Rosenfeld is a cardiologist and clinical professor of medicine at New York Hospital–Cornell Medical Center. Here are his guidelines for good nutrition.*

Guidelines for Good Nutrition

When I was a medical student, I was never taught anything about nutrition. That was left to the handful of dieticians in the hospital or to vocal consumers, largely untrained, each of whom had their own idea about what people should eat. Today, there is a department of nutrition in every major medical school in the country. Most doctors will tell you that your diet should contain enough vitamins, trace minerals, calcium, protein, fiber, and carbohydrates. They'll also warn you about the hazards of excessive fat, cholesterol, salt, MSG, sulfites, or other food additives. The modern American diet reflects these new recommendations, and more and more of us are always searching for recipes that embody them—yet are tasty as well.

The following basic principles are inherent in virtually every recipe in these pages. They reflect the current consensus in medicine that:

1. Regardless of content, the number of calories you consume will determine how successfully you're able to control your weight. Lean is "in," obese is "out."
2. Cholesterol intake should be drastically reduced in order to prevent the development of the progression of hardening of the arteries. So the emphasis here is on fish, fruit, and vegetables.
3. All fats are suspect because of their relationship both to cancer (especially of the bowel and heart) and to heart disease (even though olive oil with its favorable impact on cholesterol levels has recently been given good marks).
4. Smoked, grilled, and pickled foods should be kept to a minimum because of their demonstrated relationship to stomach cancer. That is not to say that the summer Sunday barbecue must be abandoned.
5. If you're black, have a strong family history of high blood pressure, or are hypertensive yourself, you're better off using no more salt than

you need to make your food "acceptable." Put a flower in your salt shaker and use it for decorating the table.

6. Get into the habit of eating some fiber every day. It will certainly prevent constipation, it may lower your cholesterol level, and it may possibly prevent bowel cancer.

7. Don't worry about pasta and potatoes. They're okay. It's the butter and cream you add to them that puts on the pounds and is bad for your blood fat level.

8. Eggs are a wonderfully balanced food, but you probably ought to limit them to no more than four per week (and remember that most of the cakes and pastries you buy contain eggs in abundance).

9. If you try to lose weight and lower your cholesterol by avoiding dairy products, make sure you're getting enough calcium to prevent osteoporosis—from supplements, if necessary.

10. Women who are losing iron during their menstrual periods should eat plenty of leafy green vegetables. Spinach can be delicious!

11. Vitamins are no substitute for food. Your daily requirements should come from a plate, not a bottle.

12. As you get older, you should eat less protein and emphasize carbohydrates instead.

There's never complete agreement about anything in life, especially where medicine is concerned, but most doctors will endorse the guidelines I have listed above.

* * *

Amy Barr, a registered dietician, a member of the Food and Nutrition Council of greater New York, and executive editor-at-large of McCall's *magazine, has visited the show many times over the past eight years. A few years ago, when she was the spokesperson for* Good Housekeeping *magazine on topics relating to foods and their nutritional effects, she presented a segment on safe food handling and freezing leftovers. That segment received a great response from our audience, and we've decided to reprint some of her information here.*

Good Housekeeping's Tips About Food Handling, Package Dating, and Freezing Main Dishes

The Better-Safe-Than-Sorry Food Storage Charts

SAFE FOOD HANDLING

Take some simple precautions when preparing food for storage. Always work with well-scrubbed hands and be sure all utensils, cutting boards, etc. are absolutely clean. Then keep food either hot (above 165°F) or cold (below 40°F), never in between for any length of time. Here's why: There are common bacteria present all around us that are normally not troublemakers, but can become dangerous if they are given the ideal "breeding" climate, between 60°F and 125°F, in which they quickly multiply to dangerous levels and can cause food poisoning. *Never* leave foods in this "danger zone" for more than two hours.

FOODS THAT NEED SPECIAL CARE

Take extreme precautions with foods that are especially susceptible to bacterial growth—poultry, fish and seafood, meat, creamed mixtures, mayonnaise, puddings, stuffings. Some safe-handling tips:

· Never stuff poultry the night before you roast it—the stuffing may not reheat to a temperature high enough to kill any harmful bacterial growth.
· When refrigerating leftover poultry and stuffing, remove the stuffing from the bird and store in separate dishes.
· Use cracked eggs only if they are to be thoroughly cooked, to kill any bacteria that may have gotten into the egg from the shell.

TO REFREEZE OR NOT TO REFREEZE?

You can safely refreeze virtually any partially thawed food as long as it still has ice crystals and has been held no longer than one or two days at refrigerator temperatures. Many foods, however—ice cream and uncooked baked goods, for example—will deteriorate in texture and taste.

Meat, fish, and poultry you've thawed in the refrigerator may be refrozen within twenty-four hours of defrosting. But combination dishes—pies, stews, casseroles, etc.—that have been thawed should not be refrozen.

With the exception of fruit and juice concentrates, foods thawed accidentally in the freezer over a period of days (because of power failure) should not be refrozen unless they still have ice crystals. If food is completely thawed (on purpose or by accident), warmed to room temperature, and left for more than two hours, throw it out (the exceptions: fruit and juice concentrates which ferment when spoiled, thus preventing the growth of harmful bacteria). Discard any fruit whose flavor is "off."

THE DIFFERENCES IN PACKAGE DATING

More and more foods are being sold now with a date that tells you something about their freshness. But just what does it tell you? That depends on the kind of food. Here are the most frequently used dates and what they mean:

Fresh meat and fish are dated with "date of pack or manufacture," which refers to when the food was packed or processed for sale.

Dairy and fresh bakery products are labeled with a "freshness, pull, or sell by" date, which refers to the last day the food should be sold. The date allows you a reasonable length of time to use the food.

Frozen foods, fried snack foods, cereals, canned foods, macaroni, rice, and other foods are labeled with a "use before" or "best if used by" date, after which the food is no longer at its best, but can be used safely.

Yeast and unbaked breads are labeled with an "expiration" or "use by" date, after which the food is no longer acceptable for consumption. It should not be bought or—if you already have it—used.

25 TIPS ON FREEZING MAIN DISHES

Ever wish you could reach into your freezer and pull out a home-cooked family meal, ready to heat and serve on hectic days? If you have a freezer, you can. Try this: Once a month or so, spend an afternoon or evening preparing, cooking, and freezing main dishes. Many freeze-ahead recipes call for economical ingredients, so you can save money, too. Here are tips on planning, selecting, preparing, and reheating main dishes that can add versatility and convenience to future busy-day meals.

Plan ahead to make the venture a success, not an expensive failure. Before you start, remember:

1. Don't attempt long-term storage of main dishes unless your freezer will hold a temperature of 0°F or lower.
2. Plan to use prepared foods within two to three months for best quality. Food stays safe to use, but quality declines perceptibly after six months.
3. Freeze in meal-size or individual portions. One pint usually makes one or two servings; one quart, three or four.

   Select recipes and ingredients you know your family likes, and ones that can be made in economical large quantities, using ingredients that retain flavor and texture when frozen. Also:
4. Use only the freshest ingredients—especially meats, poultry, fish, and vegetables; food can only be as good as the ingredients.
5. Take advantage of supermarket "specials" to buy ingredients for freeze-ahead dishes.
6. Choose main dishes, such as stuffed cabbage, spaghetti sauce, chili con carne, and casseroles, that can be made efficiently in large quantities.
7. Prepare meat loaves in quantity, shape into individual or family-size loaves, and freeze either before or after baking.
8. Freeze chunks of cooked chicken or turkey to be used for salads or casseroles; condense and freeze stock for chicken soup and stews.
9. Make homemade tray-type dinners in purchased trays or ones you've saved. Place cooked food in washed trays; cover tightly with heavy-duty foil to freeze. Leftover turkey, mashed potatoes, and vegetables or pot roast with gravy, noodles, and a vegetable make good tray-type dinners.

10. Don't emphasize the use of carrots, potatoes, and celery in frozen main dishes, as they tend to soften in texture on freezing.
11. Expect some changes in seasoning levels of frozen dishes. Some seasonings intensify; others fade. Many sauces such as spaghetti sauce mellow in flavor, and can be seasoned to taste when reheated.
12. Expect some separation of flour-thickened sauces and gravies. Stir during reheating to return them to a smooth consistency.

Prepare and cook most foods as you usually would, but:

13. Undercook foods slightly (especially pasta and vegetables) to allow for the additional cooking they'll get when reheated.
14. Don't include crumb or cheese toppings before freezing. Crumb toppings tend to sink and get soggy; cheese dries on freezing. Add these toppings before reheating.
15. Freeze meat and poultry pies before baking. Pie pastry (especially topping) is flakier if frozen unbaked; then bake during reheating.

Wrap and freeze prepared main dishes as you would any food for freezing. Remember to:

16. Put only cold foods in the freezer. To cool hot food quickly: Spoon food into freezer containers; place uncovered in an ice bath; stir regularly until outside is cool to the touch. Dry outside; cover tightly; freeze quickly in the coldest part of freezer.
17. Don't put more than a few containers of unfrozen food into the freezer at one time—the food won't freeze quickly enough.
18. Allow enough "headroom" in the container for expansion during freezing—approximately one-half inch per pint of food.
19. Separate quantities of individual hamburgers with folded sheets of waxed paper or plastic wrap, then wrap together with heavy foil or freezer bags.
20. Place cooled food in moisture- and vapor-proof packages. Plastic containers with tight-fitting lids, heavy-duty foil, freezer bags, wrap, or paper will keep flavors in and protect against freezer burn and dehydration.
21. Don't use waxed paper, regular-weight foil, or plastic film (except Saran Wrap), lightly waxed cottage cheese or ice cream containers for long-term storage.
22. Spoon one-dish meals and sauces into a saucepan or casserole lined with foil. After spooning in cooked mixture, cover and freeze. Then remove from pan, wrap completely, and return molded food to freezer. To prepare, peel off foil and reheat in container used to mold the dish.

Reheat main dishes without thawing, using the following methods for best results:

23. Place frozen stews or sauces in a skillet or saucepan on range top.

Add a little water to prevent sticking, and heat, stirring occasionally.

24. Heat frozen tray-type dinners in a 350°F oven for about 45 minutes.

25. If necessary, thaw main dishes overnight in the refrigerator for faster reheating in oven or on range top. If possible, stir mixed dishes regularly to assure even reheating.

* * *

Audrey Tittle Cross has a master's degree in nutrition and was formerly coordinator for human nutrition policy for the United States Department of Agriculture. In her book entitled Nutrition for the Working Woman, *Audrey addresses the 42 million women who work outside the home and also carry the responsibility for family nutrition. Here is an excerpt from that book about dairy products and the substitutions you can make to cut calories.*

Dairy Product Substitutions to Cut Calories

Substituting low-fat dairy products for their fat cousins can save tons of calories. If a recipe calls for whole milk, substitute low-fat or skimmed. I substitute reconstituted nonfat milk because it also saves money.

If the recipe calls for heavy cream or half-and-half, substitute either evaporated whole or evaporated skimmed milk, undiluted. Again, evaporated milk is a staple in my cabinet. When unexpected guests arrive, I can always whip up a quiche using leftover vegetables and evaporated milk. You just follow a basic quiche recipe, substituting whole or skim evaporated milk for the cream or sour cream called for in the recipe.

Low-fat yogurt is a great substitute for sour cream in dips, sauces, and gravies. It has a slightly tarter flavor which may call for more seasonings to balance its bite. It also separates when used in cooked recipes. To overcome this, make a roux of cornstarch and yogurt and stir into the cooking sauce. It should smooth out.

Low-fat cottage cheese can replace ricotta in casseroles. My husband, who is Italian-American, does not notice the difference. I also make a "mock" egg salad filling for his sandwiches from low-fat cottage cheese with a bit of grated cheddar cheese, turmeric, pepper, chopped celery, and onions.

Several low-fat margarines, mayonnaises, and salad dressings are available. Diet margarines have half the calories of regular margarine. They are made by whipping water into margarine. Do not attempt to bake with them. The water content makes them unsuitable for substitution in baked goods. Low-calorie salad dressings and mayonnaiselike products (usually called sandwich spread) contain almost half the number of calories as do their fat-filled counterparts.

DAIRY PRODUCT SUBSTITUTIONS TO CUT CALORIES

Substitute	For	Calories Saved
1 cup 1% fat milk	1 cup whole milk	50
1 cup skim evaporated milk, undiluted	1 cup heavy cream	640
1 cup plain low-fat yogurt	1 cup sour cream	375
1 cup plain low-fat yogurt	1 cup regular mayonnaise	1455
1 cup blended low-fat cottage cheese	1 cup sour cream	305
1 cup low-fat cottage cheese	1 cup whole-milk ricotta cheese	250
1 cup regular cottage cheese	1 cup whole-milk ricotta cheese	190
1 cup part-skim ricotta cheese	1 cup whole-milk ricotta cheese	90
1 cup white sauce made with 1% fat milk, 2 tablespoons flour, no fat	1 cup whole-milk white sauce made with 2 tablespoons flour, and 2 tablespoons butter	250
1 ounce low-fat processed cheese	1 ounce cheddar cheese	60
¼ cup diet margarine	¼ cup regular margarine or butter	205
½ cup reduced-calorie mayonnaise	½ cup regular mayonnaise	480

Source: "Tufts University Diet and Nutrition Letter," Vol. 2, No. 7, September 1984.

Reprinted from *Nutrition for the Working Woman* by Audrey Tittle Cross, Ph.D. Copyright © 1986 by Audrey Tittle Cross. Published by Simon & Schuster, Inc./Fireside Books.

* * *

Barbara Dixon is a registered dietician and nutritionist who appears twice weekly on WAFB-TV channel 9, the CBS affiliate in her hometown of Baton Rouge. She's also the writer and producer of Diet for Home videotapes, a unique nutrition-related home video series. When Barbara comes to Hour Magazine, *she is always prepared with so much data we never quite have a chance to get it all out in the segment. I'm glad to have an opportunity to share Barbara's valuable information with you in this form.*

Diet and Cancer (Foods That Help Prevent Cancer)

In recent years, many studies have been published to shed light on the diet/cancer relationship.

Many of you may be concerned, curious, and sometimes even confused over the reports associating nutrition with cancer.

You may also be wondering what you and your family should eat and what foods you should avoid.

Although many questions still need to be answered and research is still forthcoming, it would not hurt to eat a variety of better-quality foods and eliminate those habits which contribute to cancer formation.

With this in mind, here are some helpful guidelines to help you lessen your chances of getting cancer:

1. *Avoid obesity.* Eating sensibly and exercising regularly will help you avoid excessive weight gain. Your doctor and/or dietician can work with you to determine your best body weight and number of calories as well as nutrients in your diet to keep your weight normal and you healthy. Remember, if you are 40 percent or more overweight, your risk increases for colon, breast, gallbladder, and uterine cancer.

2. *Cut down on total fat.* A high-fat diet has been linked to higher rates of certain cancers, particularly of the breast, colon, and prostate.

   As a rule, high-fat diets are also high in calories, but little research has been done to distinguish between the impact of fat and total calories on cancer risk. While many studies have been conducted in and outside this country, scientists still say the facts are inconclusive. However, despite these uncertainties, there are still other good health reasons to keep dietary fat and total calories in the moderate range.

   The American Heart Association recommends we cut the amount of fat in our daily diet to 30 percent of total calories.

   Here are a few suggestions to help you lower the amount of fat in your diet:

   · Avoid rich sauces and dressings made with whole milk, butter, or sour cream.
   · Choose more fish and fowl as well as leaner cuts of meat. Trim all visible fat from meat and remove skin from poultry.
   · Use low-fat or skimmed dairy (milk) products.
   · Use cooking methods that reduce fat (broiling, baking, grilling, steaming, and boiling) rather than frying, which adds oil.

3. *Eat more high fiber foods.* Most experts agree, we Americans could benefit from eating more fiber. A high fiber diet has been found to help protect us against various cancers of the digestive tract including the colon.

There are still some questions as to which fibers are most helpful for us in cancer prevention and exactly how they work. There are several types of fibers we get from our food: the water soluble fibers (gums, pectins, and mucilages) which are found in plant stems, seeds, and fruit and water soluble fibers such as hemicellulose, cellulose, and lignin found in cereals, fresh fruits, and vegetables.

There is no ideal amount of fiber for everyone, because we are all different. However, generally we Americans can benefit from a diet of 25 to 30 grams per day. The best foods to include in your diet are whole grain breads and cereals, fresh fruits, and vegetables.

4. *Include foods rich in vitamins A and C.* Research has shown that people who eat a lot of foods containing beta carotene (a chemical part of vitamin A) have a lower incidence of certain cancers, particularly of the lung.

In 1972, the National Research Council issued a report entitled *Diet, Nutrition, and Cancer.* In that report, vitamin A deficiency was directly related to an increase in cancer of the lung, bladder, and larynx. However, it is not known whether the protective effects of vitamin A are due to the beta carotene, retinol, vitamin A, or some other content of green and yellow vegetables.

Our RDA (recommended daily allowance) of vitamin A for adults is 5,000 IU (international units) for men and 4,000 for women. Pregnant or breast-feeding women need an additional 1,000 to 2,000 IU repectively.

We get vitamin A directly from animal foods like cheese, egg yolk, and liver. Other foods high in vitamin A are apricots, butter, broccoli, cantaloupe, carrots, endive, beef liver, pimentos, persimmons, pumpkins, spinach, and summer and winter squash.

According to research studies, eating foods containing vitamin C is likely to lower the risk of cancer of the stomach and esophagus. Some experts' estimates indicate that adults require only 10 milligrams of vitamin C (ascorbic acid) each day to protect against deficiency. Nevertheless, the average adult RDA for ascorbic acid is 60 milligrams. Fruits, potatoes, and green vegetables are the best natural sources of vitamin C. Interestingly, the richest sources are not citrus fruits as you might have thought, but rose hips, broccoli, brussels sprouts, and green pepper.

5. *Include cruciferous vegetables in your diet.* Certain vegetables in this family—cabbage, broccoli, brussels sprouts, kohlrabi,

and cauliflower—may help prevent certain cancers from developing. Research is in progress to determine what is in these foods that may protect against cancer.

Your Food Cravings—What Do They Mean?

The next time you have a craving to eat certain foods, consider this:

The foods you crave may not be just what the body wants, but rather what it needs. In the past, cravings were once considered habits of pregnant women and "irrational gluttons." Now, however, the subject is getting some serious attention from nutritionists, physicians, and scientists.

According to researchers at MIT (Massachusetts Institute of Technology), the lack of certain chemicals found in our brain "serotonin" may be responsible for our cravings of carbohydrates and sugars. When sugar or starch is eaten this triggers tryptophan, which encourages the production of serotonin in the brain. This in turn gives you a feeling of calmness, energy, and elevation. On the other hand, when we do not have enough serotonin in our bodies we become agitated and depressed.

In an experiment at MIT, when a group of carbohydrate craves were given a drug that increases the production of serotonin, their cravings nearly vanished. Some researchers also say that overweight people do not produce enough serotonin and that is why they binge on carbohydrates. Other biochemical reasons for cravings are being studied. For example, scientists found, for reasons still unknown, that an imbalance in progesterone and estrogen levels in a woman's body can cause a condition known as premenstrual syndrome or PMS.

When a woman has a low level of progesterone, which also affects her blood sugar, she is likely to crave carbohydrates, such as cakes, candies, and cookies. Have you ever craved pickles, potato chips, popcorn, bacon, or other cured meats? Well, chances are it is really the salt you're after. The food itself simply helps provide the salt you are looking for. People who strongly crave salt or salty food may have a defect in the body's adrenal gland. This gland regulates the absorption and retention of sodium in the body, thereby maintaining proper fluid volume. People with hypertension (high blood pressure) may have a greater tolerance for salt, so they may crave more salt, too. Pregnant women are sometimes susceptible to electrolyte (sodium, potassium, etc.) imbalance and may crave salt, as well as those of us who exercise regularly and lose those important minerals when they sweat excessively.

Those persons who are allergic to certain foods may, ironically, crave the very food they are allergic to. Someone who is allergic to milk, for example, may crave milk or dairy products such as ice cream, cheese, and butter. It is felt they may have this craving because their body is telling them they need the calcium or other minerals in milk. Doctors have long investigated ice cream cravings as a symptom of iron deficiency anemia. If you simply "give in" to cravings without investigating why you are craving certain foods, you may be causing the problem of food addiction to worsen. In other words, you may become physically dependent on certain foods. Food addictions often lead to obesity.

How can you deal with your cravings?

1. Keep a diary for *at least* two weeks of *everything* that you eat and drink.
2. Visit your doctor and tell him/her about your cravings (along with your diary). Laboratory tests can be performed to determine whether a medical problem(s) exists.
3. A referral from your doctor to a nutritionist can help you plan your diet to get the important nutrients your body needs. And in addition, a referral to a psychotherapist specializing in food may be helpful, too.

Physical Symptoms of Nutritional Deficiencies

When you think of nutritional deficiencies, what is the first thought that comes to your mind? Most people think of skinny, emaciated people from some foreign country. The fact of the matter is, nutritional deficiencies occur in all countries, including right here in the United States. It not only refers to people who do not get enough protein or calories in their diet, but also to people who do not get enough important vitamins and minerals as well. Even obesity or overweight is considered a form of "mal" or "bad" nutrition.

When your physician examines you, he or she is looking for "physical" signs of disease or illness. These physical signs may be seen in our skin, hair, nails, mouth, and skeletal system. Physical signs such as brittle mails, falling hair, and skin problems are not always indicative of nutritional problems but can be caused by poor hygiene or trauma (physical damage). Therefore you should inform your doctor if this is the case.

Below is a summary of some of the physical symptoms associated with vitamin and mineral deficiencies.

Vitamin A

The eyes are well-known indicators of vitamin A deficiency. One of the first symptoms is night blindness or inability of the eyes to adjust to darkness. Another eye-related deficiency syndrome is xerosis, a disease in which the eyeball loses luster, becomes dry and inflamed, and good vision becomes difficult. Other signs of deficiency include rough, dry, or prematurely aged skin, skin blemishes, sties on the eye, ulcers of the cornea, and softening of bones and teeth.

Vitamin B-Complex

Though many of the deficiencies of this "group" of thirteen or more vitamins involve the nervous system, other physical signs include graying of hair, falling hair, baldness, acne, and skin problems. An enlarged bright red shiny tongue, full of grooves can also indicate a lack of B vitamins.

Vitamin C

Physical signs of vitamin C deficiency are bleeding gums, weakened enamel of the teeth, tendency to bruise easily, swollen, painful joints, and slow-healing wounds.

Vitamin D

A deficiency of vitamin D leads to inadequate absorption of calcium which in turn leads to not enough minerals in the bones. Rickets, a bone disorder in children, is the direct result of vitamin D deficiency. Signs are bowing of the legs, spinal curvature, enlargement of the wrists, knee, and ankle joints, along with poorly developed muscles and nervous irritability.

Vitamin E

There are many symptoms associated with vitamin E deficiency, though many are related to the blood/circulatory, heart, lung/respiratory, and reproductive systems. Not enough vitamin E can, however, cause physical signs such as baldness and dandruff on the head, abscesses, acne, bruises, ulcers, warts, and boils of the skin.

Iodine

An iodine deficiency results in simple goiter, characterized by thyroid enlargement and hypothyroidism (low level of thyroid hormones). Physically goiters are noticeable growths (enlargement of the neck).

Iron

In addition to iron-deficiency anemia, physical symptoms such as pale skin and lusterless, brittle nails may result from a lack of iron.

Phosphorus

An insufficient supply of phosphorus, calcium, or vitamin D may result in stunted growth, poor quality of bones and teeth, pyorrhea, rickets, and tooth decay.

Zinc

Zinc deficiency can cause many problems in the body, including those of the blood/circulatory system, reproductive system, and skin. Physical signs of deficiency of this mineral include stretch marks of the skin and white spots on the fingernails.

What can you do to find out whether the physical signs you have are related to nutritional deficiencies? Here are a few considerations:

1. Keep a diary for at least two or more weeks of all foods you eat or drink.
2. Take note when a symptom first appears and note the progression of these symptoms.
3. Keep a list of all medications and nutritional supplements you take.
4. Make a note of any illness you suffer.
5. Alert your doctor to physical signs. Do not try to diagnose them yourself.

* * *

Nan Kathryn Fuchs has a Ph.D. in nutrition, was co-founder of one of Los Angeles's most successful holistic health centers, and is author of The Nutrition Detective: A Woman's Guide to Treating Your Health Problems Through the Foods You Eat. *On one of Nan's visits to the show, she talked about the importance of good digestion. As Nan stresses several times, we too insist that you check with your medical doctor or other trained health care professional before you begin any type of treatment.*

The Good Digestion Diet

You are not what you eat, but what you digest and absorb. If you don't absorb nutrients into your cells, your body may lack some essential building blocks for good health. When you have deficiencies, your immune system is often weakened, making it more difficult for you to overcome both minor and major illnesses. Fatigued by overproduction of white blood cells to protect you from foreign invaders, the weakened immune system often triggers food allergies.

Although there is a direct correlation between good health and good digestion, it is rare to find mention of this association in medical publications. Digestion is overlooked in favor of more complicated solutions. In my practice, I find poor digestion is the beginning of poor health. Restoring the digestive system to a fully functioning system is often the key in reversing illnesses. It is the first, most important step in achieving good health, and a logical place to begin working with your own health.

Without a good digestive system you cannot assimilate the vitamins and minerals from your food. You need ptyalin (an enzyme found in the saliva), hydrochloric acid (HCl, manufactured in the stomach), and pancreatic enzymes. Chewing your food thoroughly is the first step in improving your digestion. This is the first time food is broken down by the teeth on its way to becoming tiny particles of energy. When you taste your food, your taste buds send a message to your brain, identifying it. Then the brain signals your stomach to begin producing hydrochloric acid, needed in the next step of digestion: "Joanna's eating a chicken salad sandwich on rye bread. You had better secrete enough HCl to break this one down!"

Having a doctor who understands the importance of having enough HCl in your stomach evaluate your condition is one way of determining a need for HCl. If you mistakenly take HCl supplementation and don't need it, you may feel a burning sensation in your stomach. Drinking a glass of water will dilute it and stop the burning. More often than not, we lack sufficient HCl, rather than have too much.

Several factors can inhibit your production of HCl:

1. Age. As we grow older, our stomach produces less HCl. This may be a natural way of keeping us from overeating, since we need less fuel as our metabolism slows down. If you are over 45, your HCl production may already be less than when you were younger, explaining why you can no longer eat everything you used to eat without discomfort.
2. Drinking liquids with meals. Water, coffee, and other liquids dilute HCl in your stomach. This cuts down the available HCl to digest your foods.
3. Drinking cola drinks that contain phosphoric acid. The phosphoric acid tells your stomach that acid is already present, and it does not need to produce HCl.
4. Stress or worry. These reduce enzyme production. If you're upset, don't eat. When you feel you must eat, choose something easy to digest, like a piece of fruit or a piece of whole grain toast. Carbohydrates, which begin digestion in the mouth, are digested faster than proteins.
5. Antacids. They neutralize acids in the stomach that are causing fermentation but also reduce the HCl in your stomach and keep protein from being digested. You may feel better, but you are only treating the symptoms rather than the cause of your discomfort. More HCl, rather than less, is often the solution.

HCl is one of the most important digestive chemicals your body makes. It is responsible for the amount of calcium and iron you absorb, since they both need an acid medium to be utilized. If your stomach is too alkaline (not enough HCl), calcium may collect in your soft tissues instead of getting into your bones. Also, when there isn't enough calcium in your blood, your blood takes what it needs from your bones. All women concerned about getting osteoporosis should be certain they have enough HCl to use the calcium in their food and supplements. Without enough HCl, iron may not reach your red blood cells, leaving you tired and anemic. In addition, HCl breaks protein down into amino acids for building and repairing muscles.

HCl also triggers the pancreas to produce pancreatic enzymes for the next stage of digestion. If you lack HCl, you may also lack the enzymes you need to further digest your food. In addition to all of this, low HCl production leads to such symptoms as gas, bloating, and indigestion.

Even with adequate HCl production, your body digests different foods at different rates. When you eat protein with carbohydrates, whether they are complex (as in grains) or simple sugars (as in fruit), the carbohydrates are digested first and stay in the stomach while proteins are broken down. Sometimes these carbohydrates ferment, causing gas and heartburn.

Nutritional programs that advocate separating proteins from carbohydrates make a great deal of sense, considering the number of people with digestive problems. In fact, while you are helping your digestive system function better it is a good idea for you to adhere to a low-stress plan of food combining. However, in my opinion the ultimate answer is not to restrict eating enjoyable food combinations, but rather to improve your digestive system so that you can eat, digest, and assimilate almost anything.

Why The Good Digestion Diet Works:

It combines a low-stress method of eating (separating proteins from carbohydrates) with HCl and pancreatic enzymes. The supplements give your body the digestive substances it needs to help you digest your food, while the low-stress diet makes digestion easier. By separating foods, you eliminate having some of them fermenting in your stomach and causing gas or bloating.

Specifics of the Good Digestion Diet:

The following food-combining information will allow your stomach to digest one kind of food before another one, needing more or less HCl, is eaten:

1. Eat fruit alone.
2. Do not eat proteins with carbohydrates.
3. You may eat proteins with nonstarchy vegetables.
4. You may eat carbohydrates with vegetables.

Vegetarians will not have a problem following these suggestions, since recent information from Frances Moore Lappé, author of *Diet for a Small Planet,* a book on protein combining for vegetarians, indicates food eaten over a twelve-hour period combines in the body to produce complete proteins.

Examples of Proteins	Examples of Carbohydrates
meat, poultry, fish	bread, crackers, chips
cheese, yogurt	potatoes, yams, sweet potatoes
eggs	corn, winter squashes
tofu	all grains
nuts, seeds	legumes
	cookies, cakes
	sugar, honey
	fruit

If you cannot adhere to a strict low-stress diet, modify it by eating smaller amounts of carbohydrates with your proteins or smaller quantities of proteins with your carbohydrates. This is not as easy on your digestive system as separating the two, but it will put less fermentable carbohydrates in your stomach to sit around while proteins are being digested. Examples of lowering your carbohydrate intake with proteins include: an open-faced sandwich with one slice of bread; small amounts of rice with sautéed chicken and vegetables; half a potato with fish or chicken dinners; or eggs with one slice of toast and no potatoes.

Examples of lowering your protein intake with carbohydrates include: two slices of toast with one egg; stir-fried vegetables and rice with a few almonds or slivers of chicken; pasta with a little ground beef, ground turkey, or tofu added to the tomato sauce; tabbouleh with a little hummus.

The low-stress diet for good digestion is often difficult for people who need it the most. They frequently eat too fast, don't chew their food well, and eat poor food combinations. If this sounds like you, you can become more aware and slowly change old habits. Here are some suggestions for better food combining:

Instead of:	Substitute:
juice, toast, herb tea	toast, herb tea
eggs, toast, potatoes	vegetable omelet, sliced tomatoes
cereal and fruit	cereal or fruit
chicken, egg, or tuna sandwich	chicken, egg, or tuna salad, hummus or tabbouleh with vegetables
meat, chicken, or fish with rice or potatoes and vegetables	meat, chicken, or fish with vegetables, or baked potato and salad, or sautéed or curried vegetables with rice

Better Eating Diets:

1. Follow the food-combining suggestions to the best of your ability.
2. Chew your food thoroughly; taste it.
3. Do not drink liquids with your meals, except wine occasionally, which stimulates the production of HCl.
4. Do not take antacids.

Supplements:

B vitamins are needed to produce ptyalin in the mouth and pancreatic enzymes and should be taken daily. Betaine, a factor of vitamin B, is often added to HCl tablets to help stimulate pancreatic enzyme production. After three months, reduce the amount of HCl and enzymes by half. If you get no symptoms within a week or two, gradually reduce them until you take none. Exceptions: If you know you are chronically anemic, continue taking HCl for six months to a year, checking your blood serum iron with your doctor at six-month intervals. When your iron is normal, reduce and eliminate the HCl.

B complex or multivitamin/mineral tablet—one to two times a day

150 to 300 grains betaine hydrochloride (HCl) after meals

150 grains betaine hydrochloride (HCl) after snacks, except fruit

60 milligrams pancreatin after meals and snacks, except fruit

Auxiliary Treatment:

Medical doctor: While there are many people who need HCl supplementation, I want to stress the importance of checking this out with a medical doctor or other trained health-care professional. If you have any question about your stomach's ability to produce HCl and your body's ability to manufacture digestive enzymes, have your doctor check it out thoroughly. This can be done through blood tests and other testing methods. If your results are in the lower end of the normal range, you might still benefit from HCl. Ask your doctor if taking it could be harmful in any way. Don't self-medicate.

Chiropractic: Your stomach may not be producing enough HCl because of structural imbalances, such as your spine being out of alignment, which could put pressure on the nerves that bring energy to the stomach. Some cranial faults (bones in the head not perfectly aligned) can cause an underproduction of HCl and are easily corrected by many chiropractors. Ask first if the doctor you speak with is familiar with these techniques.

Acupuncture: Just as drugs can slow down or speed up body functions, so can acupuncture regulate the digestive process, eliminating nausea, belching, and bloating.

Reprinted from *The Nutrition Detective* by Nan Kathryn Fuchs, Ph.D. Copyright © 1985 by Nan Kathryn Fuchs, Ph.D., Published by Jeremy P. Tarcher, Inc.

* * *

Joe Graedon writes a syndicated newspaper column and is author of the bestselling series of books The People's Pharmacy. *He is a frequent guest on* Hour Magazine *and he's always ready to report new and useful information. Together with his wife, Dr. Teresa Graedon, he has just completed* 50+: The Graedons' People's Pharmacy for Older Adults, *in which he deals in great detail with food and drug interactions.*

The Graedons' People's Pharmacy Guide to Food and Drug Interactions

Whenever you get a prescription from your doctor you need to know exactly how to take the medicine. Simple instructions like "take before meals" seem perfectly straightforward. But does that mean just before you start to eat, half an hour before, or an hour? Too often a prescription is handed out with ambiguous directions. There's no way to know that "take on an empty stomach" usually means at least an hour before meals or two hours after unless your doctor or pharmacist spells it out.

Your physician should have this sort of information at his fingertips. Nothing could be more fundamental. But you'd be amazed how little is known about the ways drugs interact with food, juice, milk, and other beverages. How you swallow your pills, though, may make a very big difference on whether they work properly in your body.

Ampicillin (Amcill, Omnipen, Polycillin, Principen, Totacillin, etc.), erythromycin (Bristamycin, ERYC, Erypar, Erythrocin, Wyamycin S, etc.), and penicillin (Pentids, Pfizerpen, etc.) are broad-spectrum antibiotics often prescribed for all kinds of infections, including those in the ear, throat, and urinary tract. They are less effective if taken with food; if you swallowed your pills at mealtimes, the medicine might not knock out your infection. Fruit juice, soft drinks, or wine can also interfere with drugs like ampicillin and penicillin. But griseofulvin (Fulvicin, Grifulvin, Grisactin, Gris-PEG) works better against fungal infections if it is taken with fatty food.

With another antibiotic, tetracycline (Achromycin, Bristacyclin, Cyclopar, Sumycin, Terramycin, Tetrex, etc.), you may only absorb half of the medicine when you take it with meals. If you wash it down with milk, only 10 percent will make it through your system. Milk can mess up other medicines as well. People often think that dairy products reduce stomach upset. But if you are taking laxatives containing bisacodyl (Carter's Little Pills, Dulcolax, Fleet, Theralax), milk can fool the pills into dissolving prematurely in the stomach, resulting in gastritis.

Iron supplements (Femiron, Feosol, Fergon, Fer-In-Sol, Ferro-Sequels, Hematinic, Iberet, Mol-Iron, etc.) should not be taken with milk either. Eggs, dairy products, tea, coffee, and whole grains can all reduce the amount of iron absorbed. But to lessen stomach irritation iron should be taken with food, and if you want to maximize absorption, make sure there's some vitamin C or meat in the meal.

Specific foods really can make a difference. People taking anticoagulant medication such as warfarin (Coumadin, Panwarfin) need to be wary of foods rich in vitamin K. If you are on this kind of drug, don't go overboard on foods like broccoli, turnip greens, spinach, cabbage, or liver, and watch out for green tea. Too much of any such foods could counteract the benefits of your drug.

And speaking of specifics, do look out for natural licorice if you are on a diuretic. Licorice can deplete the body of potassium, raise blood pressure, and is especially dangerous for somebody who is taking digitalis heart medicine. Even more hazardous is the combination of MAO inhibitors (Eutonyl, Eutron, Furoxone, Marplan, Nardil, Matulane, and Parnate) with foods high in a substance called tyramine. Aged cheese (cheddar, Camembert, Brie, Gruyère, etc.), ripe bananas, salami, pepperoni, avocados, pickled herring, sour cream, chocolate, chicken liver, and Chianti wine could all boost blood pressure into the danger zone.

When it comes to controlling blood pressure, pay attention. Taking atenolol (Tenormin), a commonly prescribed antihypertensive, at breakfast and dinner could reduce its effectiveness.

If all this sounds complicated, you've got the picture. But few physicians realize the complexity of food and drug interactions. The amount of fat or protein in the meal can make a difference for some medications, and even the type and quantity of beverage you drink might affect drug absorption. What's worse, the studies don't always agree. The most commonly prescribed drug in the country is the diuretic hydrochlorothiazide (Esidrix, HydroDIURIL, Oretic, etc.). It is also found in dozens of combination blood pressure medicines. Some researchers report that this drug is best absorbed when taken with food. Others have shown food interferes with maximal absorption. Such contradiction has led to controversy. When the researchers themselves can't agree, it's no wonder doctors and their patients are confused.

We have sifted through the research reports and talked to the investigators to pull together for you the latest information on many popular medicines and how they react with food and drink. Unfortunately, there is surprisingly little research available for most drugs. Although for many medications it does not make much difference whether they are taken with food or on an empty stomach, it is often difficult to find out. The *Physicians' Desk Reference* (PDR), referred to as the "doctor's bible," has a shocking lack of dosing information, especially when it comes to food interactions. We have gone far beyond the PDR in putting together this brochure, but there is a possibility your medication may not be included. That could mean either there's no good data or it doesn't matter how the pill is swallowed with regards to meals. Whether or not your drug is listed here you should definitely double-check with your physician and pharmacist on how it should be taken. They may have to contact the manufacturer to find out for sure.

Drugs that May Be Adversly Affected by Food

Many drugs are not absorbed well when they are taken with meals. Check with your physician or pharmacist for specific instructions. If they recommend your medicine be taken on an empty stomach, they usually mean at least an hour before meals or two hours after, generally with a full glass of water.

Although food may cut down on the absorption of heart medications like quinidine or procainamide, the Parkinson's drug levodopa, iron supplements, aspirin, and other arthritis remedies, they are often irritating to the digestive tract. Taking them with a meal might help reduce stomach upset.

In the following table you will find generic drugs in regular type and brand names in boldface. Food may adversely affect the following medicines:

A.S.A. Enseals
Acetaminophen*
Achromycin V
Amcill
Amoxicillin
Amoxil
Ampicillin
APAP
APF
Anacin-3*
Aspirin (enteric coated)
AzoGantanol
AzoGantrisin
Bactocill
Beepen-VK
Betapen-VK
Bethanechol
Bicillin
Bristamycin
Capoten
Ceclor
Cosprin
Cuprimine
Cycline
Cyclopar
Datril*
Declomycin
Deltamycin
Deltapen-VK
Depen

Dipyridamole
Dopar**
Duvoid
Easprin
Ecotrin
Eramycin
ERYC
Erypar
Erythrocin
Erythromycin
Erythromycin stearate
Esidrix
Ethril
Gantanol
Gantrisin
HCTZ
Hydrochlorothiazide
HydroDIURIL
INH
Isoniazid
Keflex
Laniazid
Larodopa**
Larotid
Ledercillin VK
Levodopa**
Levothroid
Lincocin
Mineral oil
Mysteclin-F

Nadopen-V
NegGram**
Nizoral
Nor-Tet
Noroxine
Norpanth
Nydrazid
Omnipen
Oretic
Oxacillin
Oxytetracycline
P-I-N Forte
Panmycin
Penapar VK
Pencillamine
Penicillin G
Penicillin V
Pentaerythritol tetranitrate
Pentids
Pentol
Pentritol
Pen-Vee K
Peritrate
Persantine
P.E.T.N.
Pfizer-E
Pfizerpen-A
Pfizerpen-G
Pfizerpen-VK
Phenacetin
Polycillin
Polymox
Principen
Pro-Banthine
Procainamide**
Procan SR**
Pronestyl**
Propantheline
Prostaphlin
Retet
Rifadin

Rifamate
Rifampin
Robitet
Rondomycin
SK-Ampicillin
SK-Erythromycin
SK-Penicillin G
SK-Propantheline
SK-Soxazole
SK-Tetracycline
Sulfamethoxazole
Sulfisoxazole
Sumox
Sumycin
Supen
Synthroid
Tao
Teebaconin
Tenormin
Terramycin
Tetra-C
Tetracap
Tetracycline
Tetracyn
Tetrex
Theo-24
Theo-Dur Sprinkle
Tolectin**
Totacillin
Trimox
Tylenol*
Unipen
Urecholine
Uri-Tet
Urobiotic
Uticillin VK
Utimox
V-Cillin K
Veetids
Wyamycin S
Wymox

*Absorption of acetaminophen is delayed by food. For quick relief, take without food.
**If stomach upset occurs, take with food.

Drugs that are Less Irritating or Better Absorbed with Food

Many medicines are so irritating they can really mess up your stomach or make you feel yucky. Although food may occasionally reduce absorption, it can often cut down on irritation to the digestive tract. Some drugs (appearing below in ALL CAPITAL LETTERS) are best absorbed when they are taken with food. If you are supposed to take your medicine "with meals," that means just before, during, or right after you have eaten. Be sure to check with your physician or pharmacist to confirm these recommendations. If you are given different instructions, find out why. It's easier to follow through if you know what you are doing.

In the following table you will find generic names in regular type and brand names in **boldface**. Medicines that may be taken with food include:

Acetazolamide
Adapin
ALAZINE
ALDACTAZIDE
ALDACTONE
ALDOCLOR
Allopurinol
Aminophylline
Amitriptyline
Anaprox
Anturane
A.P.C. w/Codeine*
APRESAZIDE
APRESODEX
APRESOLINE
APRESOLINE-ESIDRIX
Aristocort
Artane
Ascriptin w/Codeine*
Asendin
Aspirin*
Atromid-S
Aventyl
Azolid
Benemid
Bentyl
Benztropine
Betamethasone
Brompheniramine
Bronkodyl
Butazolidin

Cardioquin
Celestone
CHLOROTHIAZIDE
Chlorpromazine
Chlorzoxazone
Clinoril
Clofibrate
Codeine
Cogentin
Colace**
Cortef
Cortisone
DARVOCET N-100
DARVON
DARVON COMPOUND
Decadron
Delta Cortef
Deltasone
Depakene
Desipramine
Dexamethasone
Dialose**
Diamox
DIAZEPAM
DICUMAROL
Dicyclomine
Digoxin
DILANTIN
DIUPRES
DIURIL
Docusate**

DOLENE
Dolobid
Doxepin
Doxycycline
DYAZIDE
DYRENIUM
Edecrin
E.E.S.
Elavil
Elixophylline
Empirin w/Codeine*
Endep
ERYPED
ERYTHROMYCIN ESTOLATE
ERYTHROMYCIN
  ETHYLSUCCINATE
ESKALITH
Feldene
Femiron
Feosol
Fergon
Fer-In-Sol
Ferro-Sequels
Fiorinal w/Codeine*
Flagyl
FULVICIN
FURADANTIN
FURALAN
Furosemide
GRIFULVIN
GRISACTIN
GRISEOFULVIN
GRIS-PEG
Haldol
Haloperidol
Hematinic
Hexadrol
HYDRALAZINE
Hydrocortisone
Iberet
Ibuprofen
ILOSONE
Imipramine
INDERAL

INDERIDE
Indocin
Indomethacin
Iron
Kenacort
Kaochlor
Kaon
Kato
Kay Ciel
K-Lor
Klorvess
Klotrix
K-Lyte
LABETALOL
Lanoxin
Legatrin
LITHIUM
LITHANE
LITHONATE
LITHOBID
LITHOTABS
LOPRESSOR
LORELCO
Ludiomil
MACRODANTIN
Maprotiline
Marax
Meclomen
Medrol
Mellaril
Methylprednisolone
Meticorten
Metoprolol
Metronidazole
Metryl
Micro-K
MICRODANTIN
MIDAMOR
Moduretic
Motrin
Mysoline
Nalfon
Naprosyn
Navane

Niacin
Nicobid
NITROFURANTOIN
NORMODYNE
Norpramin
Nortriptyline
Oxalid
OXSORALEN
Oxycodan
Oxyphenbutazone
Pamelor
Papaverine
Paraflex
Pavabid
PEDIAMYCIN
PEDIAZOLE
Percodan
Permitil
Pertofrane
Phenylbutazone
PHENYTOIN
Placidyl
Ponstel
Potassium
Prednisolone
Prednisone
Primidone
Probenecid
Prolixin
PROPRANOLOL
Protostat
Quadrinal
Quibron
Quinaam
Quinidex
Quinidine
Quinine
Quinora
Quintrol
Q-Vel

Raudixin
Rauzide
Regroton
Renese-R
Reserpine
Rufen
Salutensin
SER-AP-ES
Serpasil
Sinequan
Slow-K
Somophyllin
SPIRONOLACTONE
Stelazine
Sulfinpyrazone
Surmontil
Synalgos*
Talwin Compound
Tedral
TEGRETOL
Theo-Dur
Theobid
Theolair
Theophylline
Thioridazine
Thorazine
Tofranil
TRANDATE
Triamcinolone
Triamterene
Trifluoperazine
Trihexyphenidyl
Trilafon
UNIPRES
Valproic acid
Vibramycin
Vivactil
Wyamycin E
Zyloprim

*Aspirin may be slightly less effective when taken at mealtime, but it is also less likely to irritate the stomach taken with a full eight-ounce glass of water or milk and some food.
**Be sure to drink at least six or eight glasses of fluid daily if you are taking this laxative.

Reprinted by permission of Joe Graedon, courtesy of The People's Pharmacy, Graedon Enterprises, Inc.

* * *

Dr. David Sobel is director of patient education and health promotion for Kaiser Permanente Medical Care Program in Northern California. As a frequent guest on Hour Magazine, *he discusses new perspectives in preventive medicine, self-care, and health promotion. His books include* The People's Book of Medical Tests *and* The Healing Brain, *and he's also co-author of a soon-to-be-published book called* Healthy Pleasures, *(Addison-Wesley, 1989) which tells why everything that's enjoyable is* not *bad for you—like eating hot chili peppers.*

Some Like It Hot

I can't say it is entirely unexpected, but the first rush is still always a surprise. Within seconds of popping the chili pepper in my mouth, a searing heat ignites my mouth. Eyes bulge. Breathing momentarily stops. Tears stream from my eyes. Each sweat gland on my brow weeps uncontrollably. All awareness of the outside world fades as my attention is entirely consumed by the fiery scream of my throat and sinus cavities. Then slowly a warm smile spreads on my lips and I utter, "Boy, that was good!"

At least I'm not alone. Since its humble beginnings in remote areas of the New World, chili peppers (aka capsicum) have spread worldwide to become the most used spice. The introduction of chili peppers makes for a tasty story. Christopher Columbus was sent by Ferdinand and Isabella to find a faster route to the riches of the East Indies, or Spice Islands as they were called. He was told to bring back gold and the treasured black pepper. He found neither. Hesitant to return empty-handed, he gathered up samples of hot chilies, a New World spice noted by the natives for its fiery taste. Though completely unrelated to the real pepper ground from peppercorns, Columbus (mis)named his find "chili pepper." Apparently, Ferdinand and Isabella were impressed, and the rest is history.

Within fifty years, Spanish and Portuguese explorers had peppered the globe with chilies. Today it is capsaicin, the pungent active ingredient of hot chilies, which ignites the cuisines of Szechuan and Thailand, provides the punch in the dishes of the Southwest and Mexico, adds the zing to the paprika of Hungary, heats up the condiments in some Japanese dishes, and fires up the curries of India.

Since so many people throughout the world crave the burn of hot chilies, it is reassuring to find that modern science is gradually recognizing some health benefits of chili peppers. Recent discoveries suggest that chilies may loosen congestion from a cold, burn up excess calories, thin the blood to prevent heart attacks, prevent some types of cancer, supply essential vitamins, and keep heads cool.

The highest consumption of hot chilies is in hot climates. At first glance, it may seem strange that people could think of eating hot chilies when the mercury climbs into the 100s, let alone report that it makes them feel cooler. Yet, chili-spiced foods can help with human air conditioning. The hot foods trigger massive amounts of sweating, especially of the head and face. As the sweat evaporates, it draws away heat from the body, producing the sensation of a cooler head.

Chili pepper may also become the next diet food. A study at Oxford found that meals laced with hot chili pepper and mustard help boost the body's metabolic rate by 25 percent, burning an average of forty-five additional calories. It is intriguing to consider that hot chilies may join bland cottage cheese and celery sticks as a preferred diet food. So spice it up!

Singing the Praises of Oat Bran

Lowering cholesterol has become a national pastime. In these days it is refreshing to learn that one way to lower cholesterol doesn't involve taking drugs or avoiding favorite foods. It is as simple as adding some oat bran to your daily diet.

Oat bran is the part of oats rich in soluble fiber (oatmeal contains somewhat less soluble fiber). It is this type of fiber which has been shown to effectively lower blood cholesterol. Including a third to a half cup of oat bran in your diet each day can lower blood cholesterol levels by as much as 10 to 20 percent. That drop in cholesterol can contribute to a significant savings in lives lost to heart attacks.

So try adding some oat bran. The dry, tiny flakes can be sprinkled over cold cereal for breakfast or made into a tasty cooked cereal all by itself. Add a third of a cup of oat bran to one cup of cold nonfat milk or water. Bring it to a boil. If you like, sweeten with a touch of fruit, raisins, maple syrup, or brown sugar.

Or you can make oat bran muffins. Two a day may help keep the doctor away. Oat bran can also be added to breads, meatloafs, casseroles, and fruit shakes. Experiment. You may be doing your heart a favor.

* * *

Judith J. Wurtman, Ph.D., is a research scientist at MIT in Cambridge, Massachusetts, and is a bestselling author of books about nutrition. Dr. Wurtman has said time and time again on our show that daily performance and energy can change dramatically through diet. In her latest book, Managing Your Mind and Mood Through Food, *she devotes an entire chapter to eating to ease stress. She claims that the right food eaten in moderation is among the most effective and safest of all stress relievers.*

Here are some tips on how to eat to ease stress in an excerpt from her book.

An Eating Plan for All-Day Stress Relief

The following food guidelines will help you stay calmer, cooler, and more collected on difficult days and thus enable you to achieve your best potential in the task you have set for yourself.

In reading through the guidelines, you will see that eating for all-day stress relief requires that you break a few of the time-honored rules of good nutrition. Don't worry about it. Adhering to these suggestions for one or even two days won't lead to nutritional deficiencies, especially if you take a good multivitamin and mineral supplement each morning.

But do keep in mind that *this plan is not meant to be followed indefinitely for days or weeks at a stretch.* If you feel intolerably stressed on most days, I urge you to seek the help of a mental health professional. It is doubtful that your problems or your performance will be helped by food.

· *Skip meals; snack instead!* When I first mention this rule to clients wanting to know how they can coast through stressful days more easily and more productively, many of them are shocked. Some insist that they must have three good meals a day or they will feel famished, which is stressful in itself. Hunger *is* stressful. But every one of my clients, after giving the matter some thought, realized that on particularly difficult days, not only do they eat three square meals, they also nibble constantly between meals.

Sound familiar? It should. Constant nibbling under stress is practically universal human behavior.

However, if you nibble constantly and eat regular meals as well, your calorie intake may double or even triple (depending on what kind of food you consume) over what is normal and healthy for you.

If a choice must be made—and it must, if you care about your weight— dispense with the meals on difficult days, and instead encourage your brain continuously to make ample amounts of serotonin by judicious nibbling.

· *Nibble on lowest-fat or no-fat carbs.* Among the very best of the minimal-fat carbs are "finger foods," which not only supply what you need to calm down, but also provide important hand-to-mouth gratification, which helps to relieve stressful feelings.

Good choices are:

Air-popped popcorn
Rice cakes
Cheerios and other dry breakfast cereals, used as nibbles
Miniature marshmallows

Stock up on them when you anticipate an all-day siege
· *Include some foods that provide oral gratification.*
Like hand-to-mouth movements, sucking, sipping, and chewing tend to calm and relax. Behavioral scientists don't know exactly why this should be so, but there is speculation that these actions and the comfort they provide are carried over from infancy. As adults, we do not suck our thumbs, but we still derive oral pleasure from smoking, sucking beverages through a straw, and chewing. Thus, low-fat foods that can be sucked or sipped or that require a good deal of chewing are important elements of a stress-relieving regimen.

For easing negative feelings related to stress, then, I advise clients to lay in a good supply of sucking foods, such as:

Lollipops
Popsicles
Sour balls

Ice chips are also excellent for this purpose. Although they won't induce your brain to make serotonin, because the carbohydrate content of water is zero, neither do they supply calories—a definite plus.

For sipping through a straw, try:

Ice water
Iced herb tea, with or without sugar
Iced decaffeinated coffee, with or without sugar
Club soda
Fruit juices

For chewing gratification, you can munch on:

Licorice sticks
Slightly stale bagels broken into bite-size pieces
Shredded Wheat nuggets
Dried fruit rolls (made of fruit pounded flat and rolled up in clear plastic)
Crunchy vegetables, such as raw snow peas, carrots, cauliflorets, celery, chunks or shreds of raw cabbage, cucumber *with* the skin. (Since vegetables are neutral foods and do not induce your brain to manufacture serotonin, they are best eaten *after* you have begun to feel the calming influence of carbohydrates.)

Morning-to-Midnight Stress-Easing Strategy

Now that you know what kinds of foods help to ease away anger, anxiety, frustration, and tension—and why—here's how to integrate them into a day's worth of stress-relieving eating.

If, like my grant-writing scientist client, you know in advance that a particular day is likely to be extremely difficult, shop for what you need ahead of time. (If you plan to spend that day at the office, you can cart everything with you—appropriately and safely wrapped, of course—and eat at your desk.)

More often, of course, horrendous days are unanticipated; they just get off to a bad start and go downhill from there. On those days that turn unexpectedly sour, you can switch to my stress-easing food plan at the point when things begin to fall apart. It will see you through and help you do a better job of picking up the pieces.

All-Day Nibble Plan

The most important point to remember about the All-Day Nibble Plan, developed to ease you through a stressful day, is that the foods are meant to be eaten or sipped *slowly*—slowly enough so that each of the following "menus" will last for hours.

MORNING TO NOON

3 pieces fresh fruit, such as bananas, oranges, apples, pears, strawberries, melon, or blueberries, cut into small, bite-sized pieces and mixed in a large bowl;

or

2–3 cups of low-calorie cereal to be eaten dry as nibbles—for example, puffed rice or wheat, Cheerios, or Bran or Corn Chex—*mixed with* ½ cup raisins or ½ cup chopped dates

or

Blend together in a blender or food processor and sip very slowly:
8 ounces strawberry sorbet *with*
1 cup strawberries *and*
1 tablespoon wheat germ
Eat with:
2–3 rice cakes, broken into small bits

NOON TO MIDAFTERNOON
Mix together in a large bowl:
½ cup shredded red cabbage
½ cup sliced broccoli
1 cup sliced fresh mushrooms
1 cup cooked pasta twists
½ cup sliced carrots
1 cup boiled new potatoes

or

Mix together in a bowl:
1 cup boiled shrimp, cut in bite-sized pieces, *or* 3 ounces white meat tuna, broken into chunks
¼ cup low-fat braided cheese or skim-milk mozzarella, in bite-sized pieces
½ cup sliced black olives
Eat with:
One 6-inch pita bread, toasted and split in half, *or* 1 toasted bagel, quartered

SOUND NUTRITION 241

2–3 cups unsalted popcorn *or* 1–2 cups unsalted pretzel sticks
Seltzer or salt-free club soda (sip slowly, as much as you wish)

LATE AFTERNOON TO MIDEVENING
1 cup clear soup (sip slowly to prolong "meal")
Nibble on any two *of the following entrées:*
1 order Chinese barbecued chicken wings
1 order shredded chicken or vegetables in paper-thin pancakes (moo shu–style)
1 order Chinese dumplings (steamed)
3–4 ounces miniature meatballs
1 cup meat-filled ravioli
1 cup stuffed shells
1 cup cheese- or meat-filled tortellini
4–5 stuffed grape leaves
4 ounces cold chicken or turkey in bite-sized chunks
1 cup potato gnocchi
1 cup plain tube pasta
1 cup tiny new potatoes, cubed
1–2 carrots, 1 red or green pepper, 6 plum or cherry tomatoes, 1 cup string beans, 1 cup cucumber, and 1–2 pickles, cut into bite-sized pieces and mixed together in a large bowl
Sip very slowly:
Hot or iced regular or decaffeinated tea or coffee; seltzer or salt-free club soda, as desired

LATE EVENING
1–2 frozen fruit bars, Popsicles, or low-fat ice milk on a stick, *or*
7–8 marshmallows, *or*
1–2 cups plain or caramel-coated popcorn, *or*
Turkish taffy or other chewy candy (Place in freezer, crack into small pieces; limit consumption to 1½ ounces every 2 hours.)

Although the All-Day Nibble Plan offers an abundance of foods, your calorie count for the day will remain about what it would be if you ate normal meals and snacks. Yes, you *can* improve your mood with food without worrying about your weight!

Again, please keep in mind that feelings such as anger, anxiety, frustration, and tension are your own emotional responses to unpleasant or disturbing situations or events, and that my stress-relieving food strategies will not change or do away with the source of your discomfort. *If stress is chronic, see a professional.* But if it is an understandable reaction to a temporary upset, then following the guidelines in this chapter will help you feel better and deal better with the problem . . . and allow you to get on with your work and your life.

Index

baked fruits Alaska, 40
Bavarian cream Jell-O, 148–49
Blonde Bombshell, 47–49
broiled fruits with peach cream,
    43
caramel walnut torte, 192
chess pie, 166
chocolate mousse, 63–64, 162
chocolate Valentine Marquise, 65
Chunky Munky Pudding Pie, 183
coffee crème anglaise, 64
fig pound cake, 34–35
golden pound cake, 169
Grandmother Frischman's noodle
    pudding, 117
homemade banana ice cream, 105
instant pumpkin cheesecake,
    29–30
Italian cheese farina pie, 170–71
key lime pie, 159
Linda Bell's chocolate cake,
    190–91
Marla's lemon peach pie, 120
New Orleans bread pudding, 71
Nikki's New Brownies, 41
Oreo cheesecake, 81–82
pecan or walnut tart, 75–77
raspberry steamer cakes, 21
Riesling-poached pears, 46–47
strava, 142–43
strufoli, 199–200
sweet potato pie, 181–82
Yam Slam pie, 124
See also Cookies
Diner Delites, 180–81
Dips:
    bean, Carrington's, 118–19
    Southwest cheese, 204–5
Dom's caponata, 112–13
Dom's seafood on toast, 112
Dussault, Nancy, 113–14

E

Ed Debevic's Diner (Los Angeles),
    180–81
Ed's burger sauce, 180
Egg(s):
    Bumper Crop, 27
    Garden Parmesan omelet, 20–21
in a Nest, 141
scrambled, 178
Zapata frittata, 26
Eggplant:
    Dom's caponata, 112–13
    spaghetti Lido, 23–24
Elyse's Chicken in the Bag, 191
Emmerling, Mary, 35–37
Enchiladas verdes, 139–40
Endive, baked sea bass with, 44
Endo, Kazuhito, 44
Eurotel St. Moritz, 44

F

Farina, Italian cheese pie with,
    170–71
Ferber, Larry, 201–2
Fettuccine with four mushrooms in
    cognac cream, 197
Fiesta scallops, 128
Fig pound cake, 34–35
Fish:
    baked, a la Provençale, 30–31
    baked sea bass with caraway,
        44–45
    Charo, with Hollandaise sauce,
        105–6
    Dom's seafood on toast, 112
    Grand Old House snapper, 87–88
    orange roughy with pesto sauce,
        187
    poached salmon with basil, 98–99
    redfish with crawfish sauce, 69–70
    salmon croquettes with béchamel
        sauce, 125–26
    salmon fillets with lemons,
        scallions, and parsley, 78–79
    spaghetti Lido, 23–24
    stuffed roll-ups, 59–60
    See also Shellfish
Fontaine, Joan, 115
Fortson, Kevin, 202–3
Fox, Samantha, 47, 116
French toast, 178
Frikadeller (Danish meatballs), 193
Frischman, Danny, 117
Frittata, Zapata, 26
Frugal Gourmet, The, 79–80

John Paul II, Pope, 38
Judge Wapner's au gratin potatoes, 163
Junior peanut ice, 183

K

KABC radio (Los Angeles), 81
Kale greens, 145–46
Kathy's micro chicken breasts and cashews, 206
Kaye, Danny, 57–59
Keh, David, 57–59
Kemp, Arlene Marquez, 203
Kemp, Jennifer, 203–4
Kerns, Joanna, 128
Key lime pie, 159
King, Alan, 129–30
Kreppel, Paul, 130
Kreschollek, Margie, 59–62
Kugel, vegetable, 28–29

L

La Belle Pomme cooking school (Columbus, Ohio), 76
La Bonne Cuisine cooking school (Austin, Texas), 30
Lamb:
  herbed leg of, 122
  Moghul, 32
Larroquette, John, 131–32
Lasagne, Tex-Mex, 172–73
Lasorda, Tommy, 133
Lasorda's linguine, 133
Lawrence, Carol, 133
Lee, Melinda, 167
Lemanissier, Jean-Pierre, 89–90
Lemon chicken, Best Ever, 92–93
Lemon peach pie, Marla's, 120
Lemon sauce:
  for New Orleans bread pudding, 72
  for roasted chicken, 99–100
  for stuffed fish roll-ups, 59–60
  tarragon-flavored, 53
Le Peep Restaurants (New York), 26
Lettuce:
  antipasto salad, 102–3
  Capri salad, 39–40

old-fashioned soaked salad, 132–33
with oyster sauce, 55
radicchio salad, 151–52
Levin, Carrie, 66
Linda Bell's chocolate cake, 190
Linguine:
  Lasorda's, 133
  Royale, 148
  and shrimp, alla Puttanesca, 116
Loring, Brennan, 181–82
Los Angeles Times, 81
Low-calorie chocolate sauce, 19
Lukins, Sheila, 62–64

M

Macaroni shells with onion sauce, 144–45
McClurg, Edie, 135
McKee, Todd, 136
Mackenzie, Philip Charles, 134–35
Ma Cuisine cooking school, 90
Madeline (of Ed Debevic's Diner), 180–81
Mademoiselle magazine, 35
Ma Maison chicken salad, 90–91
Manicotti Four Cheeses, 22–23
Marinades:
  for chicken, 157
  Paul's Marina, 205
  for rolled zucchini, 79–80
Marinara sauce, Michael's, 121
Marinated chicken, 157
Mario's meatballs with tomato sauce, 160–61
Mario's restaurant (Dallas, Texas), 160
Mark's salad, 127
Marla's lemon peach pie, 120
Marlborough onions, 181
Meat:
  Chinese sausage with shredded vegetables, 58–59
  Good Enough to Eat meatloaf, 66–67
  "Picadillo" (Cubano), 138
  Rocking Horse Ranch Texas chili, 61–62
  See also specific varieties

Meatballs:
    Danish (frikadeller), 193
    with tomato sauce, Mario's,
        160–61
Medrich, Alice, 64–65
Melon roll-ups, 183
Mexican pasta salad, 67–68
Miami melon chicken, 158
Michael's marinara sauce, 121
Mint and garlic sauce for chicken,
    84–85
Mobley, Mary Ann, 137
Modory, Stephanie, 204–5
Morel mushrooms, veal rack with,
    38–39
Moreno, Rita, 138–39
Morris, Gary, 139–40
Mother-in-Law's slaw, 208
Mother Wonderful's vegetable kugel,
    28
Mousse, chocolate, 63, 162
Muffins, jalapeño corn-bread, 36–37
Mushrooms:
    cream soup, 109
    fettuccine with, in cognac cream,
        197
    morel, veal rack with, 38–39
    porcini, alla Salerno, 169–70
    stuffed à la Charo, 106–7
    wild, cream soup of, 35–36
Mustard greens, 145–46

N

New Orleans bread pudding, 71–72
New York Times, 54
Nichols, Paul, 205
Nickinson, Ann, 66–67
Nidetch, Jean, 67–68
Nikki's New Brownies, 41
Noodles:
    Grandmother Frischman's
        pudding, 117
    Tex-Mex lasagne, 172–73
    vegetables lo mein, 97
Nut(s):
    apple lattice tart with, 91
    bread with dates and, 207
    waffles, 25
    See also specific varieties

O

O'Hara, Jenny, 141–42
Old-fashioned soaked salad, 132
Omelet, Garden Parmesan, 20–21
Onions:
    Marlborough, 181
    sauce for pasta, 144–45
Orange waffles, 25
Orange roughy, steamed with pesto
        sauce, 187
Oreo cheesecake, 81–82
O'Reilly, Kathy, 206
Oven scones, 55–56
Oyster sauce, lettuce with, 55

P

Pancakes:
    caviar blinis, 153–54
    whole-wheat, for shredded
        vegetables with Chinese
        sausage, 58–59
    See also Crêpes
Parenting magazine, 32
Parmesan sauce, 194–95
Pasta:
    angel hair, with shrimp, tomato,
        and basil, 73
    angel hair, with tomatoes and feta,
        98
    breakfast capellini, 27–28
    Carbonara, 100–101
    fettuccine with four mushrooms,
        197
    Lasorda's linguine, 133
    linguine Royale, 148
    linguine and shrimp alla
        Puttanesca, 116
    Mexican salad, 67–68
    noodle pudding, 117
    with onion sauce, 144–45
    salad, 130
    spaghetti Lido, 23–24
    spaghetti with prosciutto and
        porcini alla Salerno, 169–70
    Tex-Mex lasagne, 172–73
    tomato basil, 156
    vegetables lo mein, 97

S

Tostadas, raisin, 177
Turnip greens, 145–46

U

Uchita, Carol, 208–9
USA Weekly, 154

V

Vaccaro, Brenda, 160–61
Vallely, Tannis, 183
Van Buren, Abigail, 162
Vanilla sauce for chocolate parfait,
    89
Veal:
    à la King, 129
    à la Larry, 201–2
    Milanese, 156
    piccata, 137
    roasted rack of, with morel
        mushroom sauce, 38–39
Vegetable(s):
    Boitano, 101
    Holiday Tidbits, 51–52
    Jackee's quick vegetarian delight,
        127
    julienne, with chicken breasts,
        138–39
    lo mein, 97
    mélange of, 83–84
    Mother Wonderful's kugel, 28–29
    shredded, with Chinese sausage
        and whole-wheat pancakes,
        58–59
    Spring Tonic, 33
    stir-fried shrimp and, 119–20

summer, Bastille, 74–75
See also specific varieties
Vinaigrette, raspberry walnut,
    151–52
Vista International (New York), 44

W

Waffles, 24–25
Walnut(s):
    caramel torte with, 192
    vinaigrette with raspberry vinegar
        and, 151–52
    tart, 75–77
Wapner, Joseph, 163
Warm chef's salad, 42–43
Warren, Mary Lou, 91–92
Waxman, Al, 164–65
Waxman, Sara, 164
Weight Watchers, 67–68
Wheat-flour tortillas, 37–38
White chocolate:
    Blonde Bombshell, 47–49
    ganache of, Riesling-poached pears
        with, 46–47
Woolf, Virginia, 62
Wyatt, Sharon, 165–66

Y

Yam Slam pie, 124

Z

Zapata frittata, 26
Zara, Barbara, 92–93
Zucchini:
    fritters, 80
    rolled marinated, 79–80

Recipe Contest

Official rules:

To enter, remove and fill out the entry blank on the last page of this book, or take a sheet of ordinary paper and include on it the information requested on the entry blank. Be sure your name and address are clearly printed at the top of each page of your entry.

Recipes must be original and must be in English. Recipes will be judged on the basis of their creativity as well as their tastiness. The judges' decision will be final. The judges will be a panel from *Hour Magazine*, chosen from its regular cooks, expert guests, and producers. The winner will receive a 1989 Chrysler Eagle Premier.

Mail your entry to More Recipes from Hour Magazine Recipe Contest, P.O. Box 4400, Hollywood, CA 90028. All entries must be received by February 28, 1989. Not responsible for misdirected or lost mail.

The contest is open to licensed drivers who are 18 years of age or older and who are residents of the United States. The contest is subject to federal, state, and local laws and regulations and is void where prohibited or restricted by law. *No purchase is necessary.*

The winner of the automobile will be announced on the air on *Hour Magazine* and flown to Los Angeles to prepare his or her own dish on the show. The car will be presented on or before May 31, 1989. No substitutions for the prize will be permitted.* The winner shall be solely responsible for all applicable taxes and may be required to sign a statement of eligibility. The winner's name and likeness may be used for publicity purposes and the winner shall sign a release permitting such use. All entries will become the property of Hour Magazine and Group W Productions. Employees and their families of The Putnam Berkley Group, Inc., MCA, Inc., Hour Magazine, Group W Productions, Westinghouse Broadcasting Company, their respective affiliates and advertising agencies, and the judges and their families are not eligible to participate in this contest.

To receive the name of the contest winner, send a stamped, self-addressed envelope to More Recipes from Hour Magazine Recipe Contest, P.O. Box 4400, Hollywood, CA 90028. Responses will not be provided before May 31, 1989, or after May 31, 1990.

*An automobile of approximately equivalent value may be substituted by the sponsor.

More Recipes from Hour Magazine

Recipe Contest
Official Entry Blank

NAME: _____

ADDRESS _____
       (P.O. BOX)

_____
      (STREET)

_____
      (CITY)   (STATE)   (ZIP)

My recipe is:

(Use additional pages if necessary.)

Please mail this entry blank to:
   MORE RECIPES FROM HOUR MAGAZINE Recipe Contest
   P.O. BOX 4400
   Hollywood, CA 90028
All entries must be received by February 28, 1989.
The judges' decision will be final.
You may use a sheet of ordinary paper as an entry blank, but please be sure
to include your name and address on it. *No purchase necessary.* Void where
prohibited by law. See contest rules for details.